What About The Rapists?

Anarchist Approaches to Crime and Justice

Dysophia 5

Dysophia #5

Originally published by Dysophia,
Leeds, UK. September 2014

Second edition published by Active Distribution,
London, UK. March 2017

Third edition published by Active Distribution
Croatia, March 2020

Fourth edition published by Active Distribution
Croatia, July 2021

This edition published by Active Distribution
Croatia. January 2023

ISBN 978-1-909798-55-7

www.activedistribution.org

Contents

This zine looks at contemporary anarchist theory and practice on crime and justice, though it won't be using these terms. The first half will be a critical examination of Transformative Justice-based accountability processes, an approach with origins in US anarchist circles now taking seed in parts of Europe. The other half looks at retributive approaches, such as survivor-led direct action against rapists.

On Crime argues that we need to reconsider what we understand as problem behaviour before searching for solutions. In doing so, it attempts to lay the conceptual ground for the subsequent discussions.

Beautiful, Difficult, Powerful presents an accountability process in detail. It is a zine in its own right and has been taken from the book The Revolution Starts at Home: confronting intimate violence within activist communities.

Accounting for Ourselves gives an excellent overview of the history and difficulties of accountability processes. Written by the anarchist collective, CrimethInc, it is very much rooted in US punk and DIY culture.

"Anarchist" rapist gets the bat and Communiqué are statements written by groups in the US who've taken direct action to physically confront their rapists.

Beyond Revenge & Reconciliation seeks to draw together the points of disagreement and lessons learnt to help develop a pragmatic and anti-dogmatic approach to dealing with oppressive behaviour in our communities.

On Crime

By (A)legal

The title of this zine comes from a question frequently asked of anarchists. The question presents a powerful challenge to anarchist ideas, as we have neglected to engage meaningfully with the issue in favour of idealised notions of a post-capitalist, anarchic future. The concern should not be restricted to rapists and other sexual offenders, but understood to encompass other forms of abusive behaviour such as domestic violence, child abuse and animal abuse. As we'll see later, most acts currently considered crimes have been left out of this piece, either because they are relatively minor and can be addressed without too much difficulty, or wouldn't be understood as a problem or a 'crime' in the absence of the state. The vast majority of offences come under these last two categories; consider, for example, possession of a bladed article, fraud, or failure to observe conditions of leave to remain in a country – to cite just a few examples.

Why we need to talk about crime

Yet the fact that many of today's offences would not be understood as a problem under anarchy does not excuse our failure to develop practical mechanisms for dealing with unacceptable behaviour. Despite the enormous scale of problems like gendered violence, anarchist responses are all too often either evasive, kneejerk, or otherwise woefully inadequate. A common response when asked about what we would do is to simply repeat the trite refrain that most crimes would not be seen as such in anarchist terms (e.g. in a society without property, fraud, theft and so on would no longer exist), while other crimes (e.g. rape and intimate partner violence) would be rare due to the strong and supportive social bonds and the radically different values that anarchism entails; i.e. a robust critique of gender, sexual norms and hierarchy in general. All this is true, but it is delusional to think that this implies a world without transgressions or oppressive behaviour.

Far from being a hermetically-sealed system, capitalism is a culture or constellation of cultures; an amalgam of values, desires and practices that affect how we relate to ourselves, each other, and other species with whom we share this planet. Racism, patriarchy, and overexploitation of the land can equally be found in cultures that would not otherwise be understood as capitalist.

Post-capitalist or non-capitalist societies would not be static entities, either, but dynamic worlds in a state of perpetual growth and ongoing struggle against deeply incorporated capitalist desires and practices. The so-called 'overthrow of capitalism' entails nothing less than financial collapse and a constant struggle against capitalist values. As such, even in a world without capitalism as an economic system buttressed by property law, we will still have to contend with unlearned oppressive behaviour, as well as issues we may feel we have little control over. These include abusive behaviour rooted in biological predispositions, tendencies towards certain 'mental illnesses', or inferiority complexes; and conflicts driven or mediated by scarcity and access to resources. Examples include conflicts fuelled by housing needs, and even the role comrades' limited time and energy play in our responses to oppressive behaviour.

Collapse of the capitalist economy and the growth of subjugated value systems - such as radical conceptions of gender and sexuality - would undoubtedly eventually diminish the scale of abuses, but this struggle against domination is, and always will be, a continual process. These oppressive behaviours are also just as much a part of the problem as government itself; i.e. our fight against abusive partners and rapists is just as critical as our fight against the sadistic, racist cops that come round to deal with them.

In view of this, it makes little sense to wait for 'our moment' – a crisis in government, the next economic crash – or talk about 'crime after the revolution'; we need to build anarchist cultures here and now, fighting acts of domination and abuse every day. This means developing ideas and practices for responding to unacceptable behaviour taking place in our communities now.

Class

Another reason we should not be dismissive of concerns about crime and criminal justice is that these issues overwhelmingly affect poor communities. Violent crime not only hits the poor hardest, but provides an excuse for social cleansing in which all those that cannot be readily incorporated into the capitalist system of docile workers and consumers are dumped in our ever-expanding prison system.

Race

The criminal justice system also serves as the executive arm of the racist state. In the US, the country with the world's largest - and greatest per capita - prison population, and an archetype for Britain and its other neoliberal friends, one third of African American men are either in prison, on probation or on parole. Here in the UK, the picture is not much brighter; black people are seven times more likely to be stopped and searched than their white counterparts, and make up 15% of the prison population despite representing just 2.2% of the overall population.

Patriarchy

As an anarchist, I'm against prisons, not least because they're anti black and poor. But if we believe in solidarity and the unity of struggles, then we (collectively - men included) need to be working on radical alternatives to prison that seek to address every woman's fear of gendered and sexual violence, harassment, and intimidation, because these plagues are our daily reality.

Reframing how we think about crime

Key to broaching this issue from an anarchist perspective is to question all assumptions about what we think we know on crime, law and justice. This means both evading the trappings of mainstream analyses and sidestepping the dogmas of radical discourses. Here, I present some common ways of characterising the problem, with a view to developing an conceptual framework that can be used for anarchists trying to navigate this issue.

"Crime"

Crime is the term used by the state to designate behaviour it will not tolerate. Legally speaking, a crime in English law is considered an injury or harm to the state, represented in the Crown. The state then assumes responsibility for dealing with the offence, from arrest and trial to sentencing. All power and agency is removed from the victim, community, and defendant and handed over to professionals. The process of trial and sentencing can be traumatic for both victim and offender and unsatisfying for the victim. The criminal justice system cuts off an entire section of society – a marked, criminal class – who then struggle to be 'rehabilitated' into the world outside.

The notion of crime is used to create fear and division and in turn serves a multitude of desires of the powerful. For instance, criminalising property damage and disorder creates a safe environment for investors, allowing capitalism to thrive. Criminalising migration by the poor maintains the integrity of borders (and thus the state), sustaining the class system and extreme wealth accumulation. The indefinite domestic terror threat justifies military campaigns abroad, while being hardline on crime in general serves as a distraction from the root causes of social problems, and is a guaranteed vote winner as a result. Control over the definition of crime protects the theft of the commons and a string of otherwise indefensible actions by the powerful. Anarchist visions of unacceptable behaviour differ radically from the concept of crime, so no radical approach should be using the term to imagine and build an alternative reality. There are many extensive critiques of the concepts of law and crime (try Kropotkin for starters), so they won't be explored further here.

"Transgressions"

A transgression is the violation of a social norm. For anarchists this can be a useful way of characterising the problem, as it sidesteps current legal conventions and emphasises the subjective nature of standards of acceptable behaviour. At the same time, we anarchists reject many social norms, and transgression is necessary to resist oppressive cultures. A transgression in itself therefore shouldn't be seen as a problem, so this doesn't particularly help us identify problematic behaviour.

“Violence”

The principal focus of many groups exploring alternatives to the cops and courts, has been that of violence or harm, and on developing ‘anti-violence strategies’. Yet this problematisation of violence is rooted in a liberal approach that either fails to see transgressions in the context of structural oppression, or uses inconsistent logic in thinking about our struggles. For example, a considerable number - if not majority - of anarchists would support revolutionary violence against the state and capital, or against fascists or homophobic aggressors. Yet, for some reason, many also reject the use of violence or coercion against those who assault their partners, those who rape, and those who abuse. There seems to be a failure to appreciate the fact that those acts too are often rooted in systems of domination that must be destroyed. These double standards suggest at best unjoined up thinking, at worse, a relegation of patriarchy to a place of secondary importance. Further, this negation of violent or coercive responses to rape is perpetuated by two prevailing beliefs: a) the idea that retribution is harmful for victims and perpetrators, and b) the idea that retaliation makes the victim ‘as bad as the perpetrator’.

Another problem, is that the word ‘violence’ has come to be used in broad terms to incorporate omissions (such as the ‘violence’ of passivity), and even language or ideas that have the potential to cause harm or discomfort to others (witness recent debates around accountability processes in the US). This is another reason I find violence an unhelpful focus of analysis for anarchists.

It's not violence that should be seen as the determinant factor in anarchist ethics, because there is also a violence that liberates, and because many of us see violence as playing an essential part in the struggle against the state and capital; we have a strong history of using tactics that could be considered violent. Instead, we should continue to understand these problems as issues of power, and we should seek to develop responses to domination, or abuse of that power.

"Domination"

Domination is described by Michel Foucault, as relations that are 'fixed in such a way that they are perpetually asymmetrical and allow an extremely limited margin of freedom'. In other words, domination is not merely the fleeting exercise of power over others – which, it could be argued, we all do in some form or another in our social interactions. Instead, domination is the exercise of considerable control over others – and can be understood as much in individual terms (e.g. over the course of a certain relationship, a woman has come to wield considerable control over her male partner), as in systemic terms (a man coerces his female partner into sex on one occasion, in the context of a patriarchal society in which male control over women is widespread).

Re-framing crime as a fight against domination allows us to

re-orient our focus towards structural inequalities, corresponding with anarchist principles. Its does, however, suffer the shortcoming that not everything that we would oppose necessarily fits neatly into structural or fixed patterns of control.

"Abuse of power"

Approaching the issue in terms of the abuse of power, on the other hand, meets this need. We don't have a problem with power as such, but oppose its misuse and abuse to perpetuate systems of domination. Abuses cover acts of aggression which don't necessarily fit neatly into any 'category' of structural domination such as racism, homophobia and so on. A good example of this is a mugging, which might involve the perpetrator(s) exploiting their superior strength, size or numbers. The perpetrator is in a position of power, which may not necessarily (or should have to) fit within our understanding of systemic oppression, and that power (e.g. superior size), has been exploited. Yet this can of course intersect with structural inequalities, such as the expropriation of wealth by the poor. All factors will therefore need to be taken into consideration in any given case.

Conclusion

When navigating the minefield of 'crime' and 'justice' then, we need to critically consider how we understand problem behaviour. Rather than thinking in terms of crime or violence, both of which perpetuate liberal and statist discourses, an anarchist approach should be concerned with issues of power. Broaching the problem in dual terms of acts of domination and abuses of power accomodates both a systemic understanding of oppression and the exploitation of superior power in a given moment.

PART 1: TRANSFORMATIVE JUSTICE

Accountability processes, examined in detail in the next section, are grassroots, dialogue-based responses to abuses of power founded on principles of Transformative Justice ('TJ'). While not a fully-fledged theory, TJ has origins in some indigenous practices, mediation work, and Restorative Justice ('RJ'), which it closely resembles. Like RJ, it strongly opposes punitive responses to crime, places the parties in conflict at the centre of the process, and is (in theory at least), voluntary. Like RJ, it facilitates understanding between individuals, and allows them to agree steps to 'repair' the harm caused. However, TJ advocates have rightly accused Restorative Justice of being coopted by the state, which undermines its potential to challenge structural inequalities. For instance, in the case of domestic violence, restorative justice at best 'restores' both parties to the unequal positions they held before the abuse took place.

A number of groups and NGOs have claimed allegiance to TJ, despite it remaining theoretically very underdeveloped. Some groups, like Generation FIVE – whose mission it is to tackle child sex abuse without recourse to the criminal justice system – have also identified with Transformative Justice and have developed their own understanding of it, discussed in the CrimethInc article.

In the US over the past decade, a number of radical communities and projects have been experimenting with one transformative technique to have emerged: accountability processes. These ideally assume the following form: a person makes an allegation; a handful of people form a support group for that individual; the support group convenes a process and organises a similar support group for the 'perpetrator', who will be asked to broach the issue with this individual; the 'perpetrator' agrees to participate in a process; the two groups gather in a session run by a 'neutral' facilitator, during which both sides are given time to discuss their feelings; the 'perpetrator' acknowledges responsibility and an agreement is reached on steps they will take to repair the harm, such as informing future partners about what happened, or attending counselling; the 'perpetrator' abides by the agreement and is regularly checked in on by their support group, as is the 'survivor'.

As this very brief overview might indicate, there can be a lot of problems associated with such processes - from the language used, to the assumption that the allegations are always true. These processes have unsurprisingly caused considerable conflict in many quarters, but could bear beautiful fruit if executed well. This has been just a brief introduction; more about TJ and accountability processes will become clear throughout the rest of this zine. Specifically, a detailed model of such a process can be found in the following article.

Beautiful, Difficult, Powerful: ending sexual assault through transformative justice

The Chrysalis Collective

The Chrysalis Collective formed when a friend and member of our community experienced acquaintance rape by another local activist. "Diane" was a woman of color involved in several local organising projects. Through her activism, she befriended "Tom", a white male grassroots organizer working full time in primarily poor, people of color communities. As their friendship grew, Tom expressed his romantic interest. Diane made it clear to Tom that she was both unavailable and uninterested. A few months later, Diane felt that Tom betrayed their close friendship by manipulating her into sexual situations that she did not want. Their friendship abruptly ended. After several months of confusion and anxiety, Diane painfully realized that she had experienced acquaintance rape.

Aware that the state and its prisons are the biggest perpetrators of violence against our communities, Diane looked elsewhere for solutions. As infuriated and upset as she was with Tom, Diane knew that putting him in jail would not bring about the healing, justice, and peace that she wanted for herself, Tom, and the community. She gathered her close friends and formed the Chrysalis Collective. We were a group of womyn and trans folk of color with experience organizing around reproductive justice, queer health, racial justice, gender justice, youth issues, immigration rights, and food justice. At that time, we didn't know how to build a Transformative Justice (TJ) collective, how to make Tom accountable, what TJ models already existed, or what our next steps might be[1]. But we did believe in TJ as a path of individual and collective healing through accountability, compassion, and commitment. It was a way of creating a system of community-based justice grounded in the humanity – not the brokenness – of its members and in our creative capacity to transform and heal from living in a violent and imbalanced society. Instead of turning to the state, we drew on the strength and resources already in our community to end sexual assault and build safer, healthier relations among and between activists.

This is the story of our process, what we did, how and why we did it, what worked, and what didn't. Our story won't apply to everyone, or perhaps even to anyone, but we hope our offering to this beautiful, difficult, and powerful movement for TJ will inspire the work folks do in their own communities.

step 1. gathering: form a survivor support team (SST)

Our first step was to form a Survivor Support Team of folks who wanted to turn this community accountability idea into a reality. Diane called together a team of trusted friends and organizers. Some questions we considered were:

- Whom does the survivor and her allies want in the SST?
- What are the goals of the SST?

– What are the expectations, skills, commitment levels, and availability of the SST? What resources does the SST need to prepare and gain confidence for the work ahead?

The first meeting was a two-day gathering that included a lot of tears and tissues, visiting the ocean, and expressing a commitment to support Diane and see this nascent TJ process through to the end. During this initial meeting we also developed our initial goals for the TJ process. We created separate goals for Diane, the SST, Tom, and our communities, including:

– Help Diane seek a healthy, healing path, join a survivors' group, not blame herself for what happened, and keep a journal.

– Have Tom agree to work with the accountability team (AT) we planned to organize, seek counseling, share with friends that he is in a TJ process, and admit to the assault.

– Ensure that the SST and AT commit to a survivor-centred TJ process, recognize Tom's humanity, create a community-based alternative to the state, and eventually share their experiences with community organizers and groups.

At the time, we had no idea how we were going to meet these goals and whether it was even possible. Yet the aspirations we named when things were new, raw, and unmapped have remained our guiding force throughout the entire TJ process.

Since neither Diane nor our Support Team had much experience in TJ or accountability work, our next step was to read everything we could find on the subject. Our team spent several months learning, brainstorming, and talking about how to approach Tom. We needed this time to be intentional about our work, build our trust as a group, learn enough to move forward, and give Diane the space and support she needed to heal. There were times where we felt overwhelmed by what we were reading, when we were uncertain about what we could do, and when Diane had some rough nights. We built our trust by continuing to show up for Diane, for each other, and for ourselves.

step 2. expanding: form an accountability team (AT)

Next we began the process of forming the team that would be responsible for working with Tom to hold him accountable. Early on, the SST had concluded that we did not want to take part in working with Tom. We wanted to be able to focus on Diane's healing and also felt that we would not be able to distance ourselves enough from our anger at Tom to work compassionately with him. So we formed the AT as a separate team of people whose task it was to hold Tom accountable. First, we made a list of community allies who could be potential AT members. Since the AT would be in closest contact with Tom, it was vital to choose folks who not only believed in our definition of TJ but could also commit the time and energy, and be willing to develop the skills needed, to engage with an aggressor[2]. We asked ourselves the following questions:

– What experiences did they have with sexual assault, transformative justice, or community work?

– What other skills could they offer the TJ process (e.g., patience, clarity, compassion, political vision, commitment)?

– What leverage did they have in the community (e.g., positive reputation, community elder, financial resources, connections)?

– Would it be helpful if the AT was drawn from diverse communities across lines of race, gender, sexual orientation, class, organizational affiliation, and age? In our case, the aggressor was a middle-class, straight, white male with a pattern of not listening. We felt that an AT led by working-class womyn of color would be less effective than a predominantly white and/or male AT.

– And, finally: did they know Diane and/or Tom?

Forming an intentional community of people as the AT was key to the process of creating safe spaces for Diane and Tom, and crucial to our TJ work. For us, the TJ process was not about shaming or threatening the aggressor; it was about a deep transformation based on radical reflection, community accountability, and love.

Next, SST members contacted the folks individually on the list. Since their vocational circles overlapped so much, Diane chose to keep her and Tom's identities confidential. Without divulging identities, the SST informed the potential ally that a sexual assault had occurred in the community and that the survivor was starting a TJ process. We shared the SST's framework for rape, sexual assault, and TJ, and made sure that folks shared a similar analysis. Although most folks did not have much training or experience with a TJ process, we emphasised to them that they could still join the AT, pool their skills and learn together. At the end of our vetting process, our AT included four incredible activists who shared a radical political vision and a strong gender justice framework. Three of the members were well-respected activists in the social justice community with decades of community work and organizing experience, a few had previous experience of confronting perpetrators of sexual assault, and one was involved in ongoing prison abolition work. The majority of the AT team was white, male, and straight, reflecting our intentional strategy, and one of the veteran movement activists was a person of color. All of them knew Tom and/or Diane, and several had close working relationships with one or both of them. The AT's deep compassion and commitment guided them through the early months of negotiating their working and personal relationships with Diane and Tom. As with the SST, the AT members would progressively build on each other's strengths to create a trusting, powerful group.

After introducing the AT members to each other, the SST gently revealed the identities of Diane and Tom. As some AT members knew Diane and/or Tom, this required some time to process, especially since there was an awkward period of time when the AT knew about Tom's identity before being ready or prepared to confront him.

Around this time, the SST and Diane compiled a list of "talking points". These talking points included information that the AT could (and could not) share with Tom, i.e., a very brief summary of the assault from Diane's perspective: that the assault occurred by manipulation, not physical force, and other details. Crucially, Diane reported that this phase was extremely stressful. Sharing her story with the AT was a huge, public, and sometimes terrifying step. She felt a lot of fear, self-doubt, and anger, so the SST took extra care in supporting her process. They sat with her, listened to her worries, affirmed her commitment to healing, and reminded her that she was not alone in this difficult, but good and important, journey.

step 3. communicating: defining the relationship between teams

For each group, we outlined clear expectations and roles. However, we kept open the possibility of shifting them as needed.

THE SURVIVOR SUPPORT TEAM:

– Focused on Diane's needs and desires throughout the TJ process.

– Educated themselves about TJ by checking out resources in books/zines, on the web, and in our communities.

– Supported Diane's healing process as an individual and within the TJ process.

– Initiated, monitored, and evaluated Tom's accountability process through the AT.

– Communicated between the AT and survivor, making sure that the AT knew Diane's needs and gave Diane updates of the AT's process while respecting how much/little she should know with respect to her healing process.

THE ACCOUNTABILITY TEAM:

– Committed to a survivor-centred praxis at all times in their work with Tom.

– Educated themselves about TJ with an eye toward supporting Tom's transformation with compassion. (Our AT also had to balance taking the time to be fully prepared with the urgency of transforming Tom's behavior).

– Worked directly with Tom to achieve accountability and transformation. (As a group, they had to gain Tom's trust and commit to honoring his humanity. For example, they consistently reiterated their commitment to TJ, rather than to legal or retaliatory justice.)

– Conveyed and translated ideas and suggestions from the SST to Tom. For example, the AT developed specific exercises and discussion tactics to convey the concerns of Diane and the SST team to Tom.

The SST and AT had two fundamentally different roles, lenses, and responsibilities; yet they were connected by their shared commitment to TJ principles and by a similar analysis of the various forms of sexual violence and oppression.

Building a solid foundation between the SST and AT laid the groundwork for what was to come. Regularly scheduled communication between the teams addressed Diane's process, Tom's transformation, logistics, coordination, questions, and any other issues. Our understanding of TJ required that each perspective be balanced: the AT needed to hear from the SST to continually see their work with the aggressor from the survivor's perspective, and the SST needed to hear from the AT to monitor Tom's progress and be reminded of Tom's humanity despite the harm he committed. When the groups were working and communicating well, they formed a continuum from Diane to the SST to the AT to Tom, allowing for direct lines of communication as well as the distance necessary for Diane's healing, safety, and confidentiality.

step 4. storming & developing: create a transformative justice (TJ) plan

We found that it was crucial that the SST and AT develop a TJ plan before they approach Tom. The purpose of the plan was to outline our steps toward TJ if and when Tom agreed to work with the AT. We created a document where we outlined potential "steps" and then brainstormed ways of pushing Tom to accomplish the best-case outcome, ways of protecting ourselves from the worst-case scenario, and some of the possibilities in between. Our TJ plan included:

- Our goals.
- Ideas for how to first approach Tom.

– Warning signs of covert aggression from Tom.

– Backlash precautions (i.e., maintaining Diane's safety and using our leverage were Tom to respond by counter-organizing or trying to contact Diane).

– Establishing guidelines for meetings with Tom (e.g., building trust between Tom and the AT, and offering resources, "homework", and goals for each meeting).

– Working with Tom's accountability process, which involved overcoming denial and minimization, improving survivor empathy, changing distorted attitudes about power/privilege/gender, learning good consent and intimacy practices, and co-creating a relapse prevention plan.

The actual TJ process proceeded differently than what we had imagined in our brainstorm. Some ideas were never used, and others had to be developed along the way. Even though not everything was used, it was really helpful for the SST and AT to have thought through these issues together and anticipated possible reactions and outcomes. Our plan was imperfect, incomplete, and did change, but it was much better than having no plan at all. We drew on the good resources we already had – and embodied – to make the plan as strong as possible.

step 5. summoning: prepare for the first approach

Our AT and SST spent several months mentally and emotionally preparing for the initial approach and first meeting with Tom. The SST and AT lined up, vetted, and interviewed local resources, such as therapists, men's groups and other TJ resources. We found that local community resources for aggressors in relation to sexual assault and TJ were weak, so we explored regional and national support networks as well. We also asked:

– Where and when would the first approach occur?

– Which members of the AT would approach Tom? How would they invite Tom to the first meeting? When and how would they tell Tom that a survivor was seeking his accountability for rape?

– How would the AT communicate with the SST about the first approach?

We wanted an approach that would model concern (rather than punishment), confidentiality, and community safety while still giving us enough leverage to compel Tom to participate in the TJ process. In our discussions, it was helpful for us to distinguish our tactics for the "initial approach" when we would ask him to come to a meeting about a community concern, and the "first meeting" where we would tell him that the community concern was his behavior and Diane's experience of rape. It was agreed that two folks whom Tom respects would do the initial approach and keep the exchange brief and general to avoid tipping him off as to what the meeting would be about.

We felt that this plan would maximize our chances of getting him to the table to listen to our concerns, be willing to participate in the TJ process, and minimize any reaction that could endanger Diane. The success of the "initial approach"would rely on the fact that Tom cared about the community and would want to be part of the solution to a community problem; the success of the "first meeting" would rely on the fact that these concerns would be brought to him by people he trusted and respected, and that it would be done in a way that was not about shaming or punishing him.

Preparing for this step was important because Tom's reaction could not be predicted, and how the AT responded could influence Tom's participation in the TJ process. What if Tom refused to engage with the AT, leaving everyone unhealed and the community endangered? What if Tom freaked out when his behavior was named as rape? What if everything went as planned? We simplified our preparation for the first approach by assuming a best-case scenario, but we also developed a list of tactics to influence and raise the stakes for Tom in case he resisted (e.g., going to his friends and colleagues).

The AT chose two members whom Tom respects and who have worked directly with him. After a community event they all attended, the two members casually approached him and said, "Hello, we would like you to join us for a meeting about an important matter concerning a member of our community." They diverted Tom's questions about the community member's identity by saying, "There are issues of confidentiality. We'll talk about that at the meeting."

Neither the assault nor the TJ process were mentioned. For the first approach, we felt the less said, the more likely Tom would participate in the first meeting (where the details would come out and the real work would begin). We were wary of sharing any more information about the assault or TJ process with Tom for fear it would scare him away, trigger aggressive reactions, or turn him off. Our primary goal was to invite Tom to a first meeting, and fortunately, he agreed to attend.

Immediately after the initial approach, the two members processed the experience with the rest of the AT and SST, as everyone was anxious to know how it went.

In hindsight, we've realized that this approach had the extra benefit of activating within Tom the mental frames he and we needed for this process: responsibility, caring, trust (we were going to trust him with a community concern), at the possible cost of him feeling betrayed by our half-truth. In contrast, an "authoritative" approach would likely activate an offense/defense response in Tom so he could regain "his way" – the opposite of what was needed in the process. (And truthfully, we just felt uncomfortable acting in an "authoritative", top-down manner, rather than modeling horizontal cooperation).

Although this first invitation to the process seemed simple enough, it was an extremely stressful time for Diane, the SST, and the AT. We supported Diane and each other through our feelings of doubt and anxiety about whether the first approach and meetings would be effective. Unfortunately, we were not prepared for the growing internal stress in the groups. Our SST and AT lost some folks due to the increased intensity of the process and the time commitment. This was a time when folks already saw and felt how the TJ process would roll out.

step 6. building: the first meeting

The AT planned the first meeting with an eye towards Tom's potential responses. This would be the first time Tom would hear that Diane had experienced rape, that she had been deeply harmed by his behaviors, and that we would be asking him to engage in a long, complex process of TJ. We considered the following range of feelings that Tom might experience and/or express:

– Ganged up on. To minimize the chances of this happening, we limited the first meeting to the two AT members we had selected – community leaders and elders who modeled cooperation, not domination – to make the initial approach because among us they were the most trusted and respect by Tom.

– Denial, outrage, remorse, shame, guilt, fear, and defensiveness. With these feelings in mind, we didn't expect much at first. We set and kept good boundaries, and used active listening.

– Betrayal by the survivor and AT. We tried to build trust and safety right away by compassionately (but critically) listening to his experience, giving him space to feel betrayal and denial, and allowing him to offer some input on his TJ process.

– Overwhelmed by too much information. To avoid this we kept things simple at first.

At the first meeting, the two AT members gently told Tom that a community member experienced his behavior as rape. They revealed Diane's identity and shared a few of the SST's talking points. The AT folks explained that Diane and the community had experienced a harm which must be healed in a responsible way. These points were communicated both verbally and in a written document for Tom to reread and process later. Some of those points were:

– The AT was there to serve the needs of Diane and the community.

– The AT would support Tom in his accountability and transformation process.

– The AT would provide Tom with a simplified statement or version of Diane's experience, rather than a detailed account that could lead to a debate over what happened.

– The AT acknowledged that Tom's intention and experience might be different than Diane's.

– The AT set clear boundaries around the survivor (i.e., do not contact Diane).

– The AT valued Tom's contributions to the community.

– The AT and Tom had a mutual interest in stopping sexual assault in the activist community.

– The AT invited Tom to bring his needs and goals to the next meeting.

The AT members were also prepared to:

– Validate Tom's story, feelings, and experience, if offered; repeat our support of the survivor's experience if Tom tried to blame Diane for what happened.

– Deflect questions or challenges about the incident, violation, process, or Diane until the next meeting.

– Avoid volunteering any additional information "to be helpful".

– Ask if Tom had friends to process with afterwards.

– Establish that Tom should communicate with the AT through a predesignated point person.

After this meeting, the AT members debriefed, updated the SST, supported each other, and relaxed as best they could. Their work had just begun.

step 7. transforming: meetings with the accountability team

Fortunately, the initial approach and first meeting led to regular meetings between Tom and the entire AT. During each meeting, the AT allowed generous time for check-ins and emotional processing. As expected, our personal feelings, such as anger and judgement, arose, so we consistently re-emphasized the entire team's commitment to

TJ – not to punishment – and to building a climate of trust and respect.

In the initial meetings, the AT gave an overview of the process that we expected going forward. We solicited boundaries from everyone and developed shared goals, ensuring a place for Tom's voice in the process. We also learned not to expect much from him during the initial meetings. The work ahead was likely to be long, and we figured it was most important that each meeting lead to the next one.

As we've continued, the AT has played many expected and unexpected roles, such as supporter, friend, challenger, therapist, investigator, contract negotiator, and judge. Always, the AT and SST have worked together to make sure that the survivor-centred TJ process be guided by the goals of the TJ plan. The AT also focused on the shared goals produced with Tom. They respected Tom's needs while prioritizing the safety of Diane and of the community.

MEETINGS WITH TOM HAVE FOCUSED ON THE FOLLOWING:

– Challenging rape culture: Pacing the information slowly, starting with sexual-assault definitions and statistics; studying and discussing relevant zines and resources; repeating our understanding of rape and how it differs from the criminal definition and mainstream myths; exploring the difference between intent and impact; and challenging the primacy that rape culture gives to an aggressor's intent over the consequences of the aggressor's behavior for the survivor and the community.

– Exploring unrelated scenarios: Describing situations involving culpability, intent, manipulation, and then connecting them to the incident; asking what taking responsibility would look like even if Tom were blameless.

– Focusing on the survivor's experience: Asking Tom how something looks and feels from Diane's perspective; asking "What did you take from that statement?"; asking who got what they wanted; restating the survivor's experience; pressing for feelings and empathy; understanding the meaning and practice of good consent.

– Connecting with Tom: Connecting to his activism and using various anti-oppression frameworks that would be familiar to him; involving Tom in problem solving; pushing Tom to places of discomfort; asking Tom to imagine he is on an AT for someone else; assigning and discussing homework; practicing active listening and mirroring.

We also expected Tom to manipulate conversations to avoid accepting the painful reality that he had deeply harmed Diane and, by extension, the community.

AT members attempted to avoid this by:

– Practicing role-plays about defensive behaviors.

– Developing mantras for tough situations (i.e., "Diane experienced that as harm").

– Debriefing together after every meeting with

Tom, with a particular focus on detecting manipulation.

– Debriefing with the SST after every meeting or two to check in with the TJ process.

– Trusting the experiences and wisdom of the group members.

Throughout this process, one difficult and recurring question was whether the AT and Tom had met their goals. The AT had clear goals for Tom, i.e., that he admit to rape and seek professional counseling. At the same time, we had been frustrated by how to measure or evaluate these goals. The AT not only wanted Tom to change his language and behavior; they also wanted him to internalize what he was learning and emotionally "get it". Observing behaviors and statements were one way to measure change, but we realized that there was no guarantee that he was really "getting" it. Given the difficulty in measuring our success, it has been crucial to set clear goals for Tom from the beginning of this long process of transformation.

GOALS FOR TOM:

– LEARN about sexual assault, consent, privilege, patriarchy, gender socialization, and rape culture.

– RESPECT physical and communication boundaries for Diane's safety.

– EXAMINE his past behavior for other experiences of manipulation and assault; acknowledge and be accountable to that history; and keep the community safe in the present and future if this is repeat behavior.

– SEEK professional counseling for aggressors or join an aggressor recovery group.

– SELF-EDUCATE to deeply understand the incident, his intent, and behavior, and the subsequent harm to Diane and the community.

– DISCUSS AND MODEL consent behavior for future relationships.

– COMMIT to acts of restitution to Diane and the community.

step 8. evaluating: lessons learned

As much as we prepared, there have been important lessons that we did not anticipate in our TJ work:

– The situation – and many rapes in activist communities – involved coercion, manipulation, and/or entitlement, not sheer physical force, and reflected how deeply rape myths and culture are embedded within our own activist circles. Male entitlement, racism, and an ignorance of rape culture made it that much harder for Tom to recognize his behavior as rape.

– It was hard to balance Diane's need for confidentiality with the need to warn the community about Tom, and this remained an unresolved tension in our TJ process.

– Diane's and Tom's transformations needed to follow their own paths, which might mean that Tom might be ready to offer restitution before or after Diane is ready to receive it.

– We should have been more serious about communication between the AT and the SST. It sounded easy enough, but it sometimes felt overwhelming to schedule another meeting or call. No matter what the excuse, we have learned to make time to check in. It is worth much more than we first realized.

– The aggressor accountability process got so involved that the SST started to lose track of Diane's healing process. At one point, our meetings were all about Tom's progress, and we would run out of time before addressing what Diane needed. We are learning to put Diane's well-being back at the center of our process through things like expanding our support circle, reading zines together, and making a trigger plan. (A trigger plan is a way for Diane to identify and overcome her triggers. When she experiences a traumatic memory or reaction, the trigger plan that we developed together helps her identify what is happening and the steps she needs to take to feel safe).

The Chrysalis Collective is still actively engaged in our survivor-centred TJ process. The more we learn about TJ, the more we realize that it is a deep commitment requiring a lot of energy and patience. Our unfinished process has lasted almost two years so far and we have gone through stressful times. Yet healing and transformation is clearly, slowly, steadily happening for everyone involved. This experience has connected each of us in unexpected and powerful ways that reaffirm our collective commitment to transforming ourselves and our communities.

working definitions

– RAPE. Nonconsensual sex through physical force, manipulation, stress or fear; the experience of sex as the unwanted physical, emotional, mental, or spiritual violation of sexual boundaries; not as an act of caring, love or pleasure; sexual violation of trust.

– SEXUAL ASSAULT. Any unwanted physical, emotional, mental, or spiritual violation of sexual boundaries.

– CONSENT. An understandable exchange of affirmative words and actions regarding sexual activity; agreement, approval, or permission that is informed and freely and actively given without physical force, manipulation, stress, or fear.

suggested resources

generationFIVE: Ending Child Sexual Abuse in Five Generations

www.generationfive.org

Hollow Water: Community Holistic Healing Circle

www.iirp.edu/article_detail.php?article_id=NDc0

Indigenous Issues Forums

www.indigenousissuesforums.org (dead link)

INCITE! Women of Color Against Violence

www.incite-national.org

Communities Against Rape and Abuse (CARA)
www.cara-seattle.org (dead link)
Center for Transformative Change
www.transformativechange.org
Angel Kyodo Williams, "Doing Darkness: Change Vs. Transformation,"
Transformation: Vision and Practice for Transformative Social Change (October 2009).
www.transformativechange.org/docs/nl/transform-200910.html

notes

1. After a lot of phonecalls, web searches, conversations, and networking with amazing activists around the country, we found incredible resources. We are grateful for the wisdom and work shared by the TJ activists who came before us, especially the folks from GenerationFIVE, Hollow Water, Indigenous Issues Forum, INCITE! Women of Color Against Violence, Communities Against Rape and Abuse (CARA), and the zine "The Revolution Starts at Home: confronting partner abuse in activist communities," eds. Ching-In Chen, Jai Dulani, and Leah Lakshmi Piepzna-Samarasinha (2008).

2. The Chrysalis Collective deliberately uses the term "aggressor" throughout the chapter for reasons similar to those offered by a collective of women of color from CARA: "[W]e use the word 'aggressor' to refer to a person who has committed an act of sexual violence (rape, sexual haras-

sment, coercion etc.) against another person. Our use of the word 'aggressor' is not an attempt to weaken the severity of rape. In our work of defining accountability outside of the criminal system, we try not to use criminal-based vocabulary such as 'perpetrator', 'rapist', or 'sex predator'". See CARA, "Taking Risks: Implementing Grassroots Accountability Strategies," in Color of Violence: The INCITE! Anthology, ed. INCITE! Women of Color Against Violence (Cambridge, MA: South End Press, 2006), 302nl.

[Extract from Ching-In Chen et al. The Revolution Starts at Home: confronting intimate violence within activist communities]

Accounting for Ourselves

Breaking the Impasse Around Assault and Abuse in Anarchist Scenes

by CrimethInc.

Sexual assault and abuse continue to plague anarchist circles and spaces. In response, we've developed processes to hold each other accountable outside of the state. But why can't we seem to get them right? This essay examines the context in which these community accountability models emerged and analyzes the pitfalls we've encountered in trying to apply them. To move beyond the impasse around sexual violence within our scenes, we need to challenge the idea of community itself and take our resistance in new directions.

Introduction

"I don't believe in accountability anymore...my anger and hopelessness about the current model are proportional to how invested I've been in the past. Accountability feels like a bitter ex-lover to me...the past ten years I really tried to make the relationship work, but you know what?"

-Angustia Celeste,
"Safety is an Illusion: Reflections on Accountability"

Getting Started: Origins and Purpose

Sexual assault and abuse tear us apart. They fracture our communities, ruin individual lives, sabotage projects and organizing, reveal nasty contradictions between our supposed ideals and our actual practices, and maintain a climate of fear and oppression, especially for women.

Sexual assault is political; it is a function of patriarchy, not just an individual harm done by individual people (usually men) to others (most often women). Sexual assault and abuse, partner violence, child abuse, and sexual harassment are primary ways that men physically impose domination over women. Sexualized violence helps to maintain patriarchy, heterosexism, trans oppression, ageism and oppression of youth, racist colonialism, and genocide. The struggle against sexual assault and abuse is essential for revolutionary transformation.

The accountability process model has been one of the primary tools used by anarchists to address assault and abuse in recent years. This essay analyzes this model in hopes of provoking honest, self-critical discussion about how we respond to assault and abuse within anarchist scenes, and imagining directions to move forward.

This article is NOT intended to serve as an accessible introduction to community accountability processes; it assumes that you have some knowledge of what they are and how they work (or don't work). It draws specifically on North American anarchist, punk, and radical activist subcultures and presumes that the reader understands their context and language. If you don't, try reading some of the sources cited below [editor: at the end of zine] before this one. If you're an anarchist and you've had some experience with efforts to respond to assault and abuse within your scene under the label of "accountability," this is intended for you.

Gender Frameworks

Gender is complicated; some folks we might perceive as male or female don't identify that way, and some don't identify as either. In referring to "men" or "women," we mean folks who identify that way, whether cisgender or transgender. Throughout this essay, both survivors and people who've assaulted or abused others are referred to in general using "they" as a gender-neutral pronoun. Assault and abuse can be committed by anyone against anyone, across gender lines; sometimes cis women, trans men and women, and genderqueer folk assault, and often cis men are survivors as well. But this acknowledgment should not erase the fact that the vast majority of folks who abuse and assault are cis men, and the majority of folks they abuse and assault are women.

Sexual assault and abuse are neither gender-specific (i.e., they can only happen by or to people of a certain gender) nor gender-neutral (i.e., the gender of a person who assaults or is assaulted is irrelevant to the conversation). We must understand the gendered patterns of assault and abuse as an expression of patriarchal domination, without making invisible experiences that fall outside of that gendered framework.

Restorative and Transformative Justice

In speaking about accountability processes, we're referring to collective efforts to address harm—in this case, sexual assault and abuse—that focus not on punishment or legal "justice" but on keeping people safe and challenging the underlying social patterns and power structures that support abusive behavior. In the loosest sense, this might simply mean a few friends sticking up for someone who's been hurt: asking them what they need, and trying to negotiate for those needs with the person who hurt them and among the community they share. Some processes involve a group that mediates between an individual and the person calling them out, or separate groups supporting each person and facilitating communication between them. These processes usually involve setting out conditions or "demands" for the person who's been called out as a means of restoring safety or trust and preventing the harm from happening again, and some method for following up to ensure that these demands are met. All of these different approaches share an intention to address the harm done directly without relying on the state.

Community accountability appeals to anarchists as a critical alternative to the adversarial framework of the criminal "justice" system. According to this framework, two parties in conflict are assumed to have opposite interests; the state considers itself the aggrieved party and thus acts as mediator; and "justice" means deciding which person is correct and which person suffers consequences—which are determined by the state, and usually unrelated to the actual harm done or its root causes. In contrast, restorative justice focuses on the needs of the ones harmed and those who did harm, rather than the need to satisfy the abstract principles of law or to exact punishment. Folks who've been harmed play an active role in resolving a dispute, while those who harm are encouraged to take responsibility for their actions and repair the harm they've done. It is based on a theory of justice that sees "crime" and wrongdoing as an offense against individuals or communities rather than the state. Many of the current working models for restorative justice originated in Maori and North American indigenous communities.

Building on that framework, the transformative justice model links restorative justice's focus on rectifying harm rather than strengthening state power with a critique of systematic oppression. According to Generation Five, an organization that grounds their work to end child sexual abuse in this model, the goals of transformative justice are:

- Safety, healing, and agency for survivors
- Accountability and transformation for people who harm

- Community action, healing, and accountability
- Transformation of the social conditions that perpetuate violence—systems of oppression and exploitation, domination, and state violence

The anarchist practice of community accountability rests in theory on these underlying principles, along with the DIY ethic and a focus on direct action.

Where We're At

Anarchist Community Accountability: Recent History and the Current State of Things

How did this set of practices around responding to sexual assault and abuse emerge? In the 1990s and early 2000s, women and other survivors responded to assault and abuse in a variety of ways, including making zines calling people out to distribute at shows, discussing their experiences amongst themselves, warning people in other communities about repeat assaulters, and in some cases physically confronting them. The Hysteria Collective based in the Portland, OR. area represented one of the early structural attempts to respond to sexual assault, producing and distributing literature, challenging the presence of abusive men in the punk scene, and organizing a conference. In other towns, folks formed girl gangs for self-defense and concerted confrontational action. However, more often than not, such efforts were isolated, belief in rape myths persisted amongst anarchists (especially men), and survivors who attempted to speak out were ignored, shunned, dismissed for distracting attention from more important issues, or blamed for COINTELPRO-style divisiveness.

In response, anarchist women and others worked to encourage anarchist scenes to take sexual assault and abuse seriously and promote a culture of consent. Much of this spread through zine culture, particularly Cindy Crabb's Doris and Support zines; also, workshops began appearing at radical conferences discussing survivor support, consent, and positive sexuality. Men's groups began to organize against sexual violence in some radical scenes, such as the Dealing With Our Shit (DWOS) collective founded in Minneapolis in 2002. A major turning point occurred at the 2004 Pointless Fest in Philadelphia, where concert organizers publicly announced that three women had been raped at the event and established collectives to support the survivors and figure out how to deal with the rapists. These collectives became Philly's Pissed and Philly Stands Up, long-standing separate but collaborating collectives devoted respectively to survivor support and assaulter intervention.

Assault, accountability, and consent became topics at nearly all anarchist conferences and gatherings. Many distros began to carry zines on the subject, touring bands spoke from stage about it, and anarchists in many other cities formed support and accountability collectives. Organizers of mass mobilizations began to develop plans for response, culminating in a full-scale sexual assault response infrastructure at the anti-G20 convergence in Pittsburgh in 2009.

So how do things stand today? Terms such as "consent," being "called out," "accountability process," and "perpetrator" are in wide use, to the point of becoming the subject of jokes. A great many people have been called out for abusive behavior, and dozens of accountability processes are ongoing in various stages. An identity politics around the labels "survivor" and "perpetrator" has emerged, with scenes polarizing around them. In spite of efforts to caution against this and encourage all participants in accountability processes to remain self-critical, these labels have sometimes been used to leverage power, dispense or deny legitimacy, and erase differences in experience.

Philly Stands Up continues their work, getting paid by colleges to lead trainings on their model and functioning as a sort of semi-formal sexual assaulter surveillance organization, with folks from around the country contacting them for updates on different ongoing processes. They networked with other groups doing transformative justice work at the US Social Forum in Detroit and hosted a three-day training for community accountability organizers in January 2011. Numerous other similar collectives have been attempted among anarchists in other cities, though few have had the longevity or prominence of PSU. As more and more intra-scene communication moves onto the internet, a number of websites (most prominently anarchistnews.org) have become major hubs for shit-talking around the politics of assault and accountability. Websites have also appeared giving information about specific individuals who have assaulted or abused others.

Most anarchist gatherings now issue guidelines about consent and sexual assault response, and often address the presence of people involved in accountability processes. Based on the policies developed by sexual assault response organizers at the 2009 Pittsburgh anti-G20 mobilization, organizers at the 2010 anti-IMF mobilizations in Washington DC posted an announcement stating "No Perpetrators Welcome." It explained that in an effort to make the demos safe for survivors, "people who have perpetrated in the past, people running away from accountability processes, and people who refuse to respect the IMF Resistance Network consent guidelines" were prohibited from all organizing spaces and events. More recently, organizers for the 2012 Toronto Anarchist Book Fair echoed this language banning all perpetrators, but added:

> *We understand and respect that communities have engaged in their own processes around these incidents. If you have gone through an accountability process and the survivor, joined by the community, feels you have sufficiently dealt with your shit, this statement does not include you.*

Likewise, the organizers of the 2012 New York Anarchist Book Fair banned:

People who have perpetrated inter-personal violence, as-

sault and/or harassment unless they are actively engaged in an accountability process and currently in compliance with all the terms and/or demands of that process (according to the facilitators, the survivor, and/or whomever's been designated to monitor the agreements emerging from the process).

A major source of controversy has been the preemptive banning of individuals who've been called out for sexual assault or abuse from anarchist gatherings. In recent years, survivors and their supporters have increasingly requested for particular individuals who have sexually assaulted others to be banned from upcoming events. Organizers have struggled to prioritize believing survivors without preemptively condemning people, and to balance transparency against privacy and avoiding retraumatization. An internet brouhaha emerged when a person online posted an email they had received from organizers of the New York Anarchist Book Fair, asking them not to attend without specifying the reason. Some interpreted the email as a Kafkaesque, authoritarian presumption of guilt through anonymous rumor, while others defended it as an effort to remain neutral while attempting to secure a sense of safety for other attendees.

While controversies persist around our methods of response to sexual assault, norms around sexuality have shifted significantly within anarchist scenes in recent years. Discourses of consent have expanded, while information about assault, survivor support, and options for accountability has become increasingly available. This has noticeably changed how we conduct sexual relationships, relate to our own bodies, and respond to survivors. Compared to previous years, many anarchists have become more conscious of sexual power dynamics and increasingly empowered to communicate boundaries and desires.

However, sometimes abusers in anarchist communities "talk the talk" of consent and support while doing the same old shit. As the author of "Is the Anarchist Man Our Comrade?" challenges:

> *Accountability processes often do a lot of good but sometimes they just teach men how to appear unabusive when nothing's changed but the words coming out of their mouth. Survivors and friends are left wondering if said male is no longer a threat. Eventually the issue recedes from peoples' minds because they don't want to seem overly reactionary and don't know what further steps to even take and the perpetrator is able to continue on in their life without much changing.*

How can we prevent these discourses from being appropriated by the sensitive anarcha-feminist sexual assaulter? It seems that the availability of community accountability processes hasn't changed the patterns of behavior they were developed to address. What isn't working here?

Ten Pitfalls of Community Accountability Processes

Two important qualifications: first, these are pitfalls of

accountability processes as they're actually practiced, as we've experienced them. Some of these pitfalls aren't inherent to these processes, but are simply mistakes commonly made by people who undertake them. One might respond to many of these critiques by saying, "Well, if people actually applied the model as it's intended, that wouldn't happen."

Fair enough; but for any such model to be widely relevant and applicable, it has to be robust enough to be able to succeed even when conditions aren't optimal, or when folks don't or can't follow the model perfectly. So bear in mind that these pitfalls don't imply that our accountability models are futile or doomed. On the contrary, because we're invested in figuring out how to end assault and abuse, we have to be unflinchingly critical in examining efforts to do so.

Second, the things people frequently say to avoid responsibility should not be mistaken for problems with accountability processes. For example: "This stuff distracts us from the real revolutionary issues; it's divisive and hurts the movement; holding people accountable is manipulative/coercive/overemphasized/a power grab," and so forth. These are not pitfalls of accountability processes; these are problems of patriarchy and its supposedly anarchist apologists.

That said, here are some of the major difficulties we've encountered in the processes we've developed to hold each other accountable for sexual assault and abuse within anarchist scenes.

1) There is no clear sense of when it's over, or what constitutes success or failure. When can we say definitively that a certain person has "worked on their shit"? What will allow a survivor and their supporters to feel comfortable with someone continuing to participate in a shared community? When expectations aren't explicit, goals aren't concrete, or the time-line and means of assessment aren't clear, confusion and frustration can follow for everyone involved.

This often happens because we have so little experience with alternative modes of resolving conflict and addressing harm that we don't know what to look for. For instance, even if a person has "been accountable," the survivor may or may not necessarily feel better. Does this determine the success or failure of a process? If someone has done all the things asked of them, but others aren't sure if the steps taken were effective, what could confirm that real change has taken place? It may or may not actually be possible to restore trust after harm has been done; if not, this may not be the right type of process to undertake.

Likewise, past what point can we agree that someone has NOT worked on their shit, and we shouldn't bother wasting our time on it anymore? Some accountability processes drag on for months and years, diverting collective energy from other more fulfilling and useful ends. One stubborn sexist can sour an entire scene on making good faith efforts to hold folks accountable—which goes to show how important it is to know when to end an attempted process before it drags everyone down with it. If we're going to invest so much time and energy in these processes, we need a way to assess if it's worthwhile, and when to admit failure. And that requires determining what failure would mean: for instance, kicking someone out of a scene, trying other modes of response, or admitting to a survivor that we can't enforce their demands.

2) Standards for success are unrealistic. For instance, the common demand that someone work on their proverbial shit is either too vague to be meaningful, or practically translates to a profound psychological transformation beyond the bounds of what we can achieve. As the article "Thinking Through Perpetrator Accountability" puts it:

> *Perpetrator accountability is not an easy or short process... It takes a lifelong commitment to change behaviors that are so deeply ingrained; it requires consistent effort and support. When talking about follow-up, we should be making schedules for weeks, but also talking about checking in after months and years. It takes that kind of long-lasting support to make real transformation possible.*

Let's be frank: if we expect people to remain involved in an accountability process for some scumbag they don't even like for years, and we expect this as a norm for an increasing number of processes for different people, who may or may not be cooperative—we are not setting a realistic standard.

That's not to say that the article is wrong; transformation of patriarchal and abusive behavior patterns is a lifelong process. But is it really a surprise that we fail to sustain these difficult, unrewarding processes stretching over such lengths of time, when few anarchists in our scene follow through on long-term commitments to even our most fervent passions? What can we realistically commit to doing?

3) We lack the collective ability to realize many demands. We can say we're committed to meeting survivor demands, but that's just empty rhetoric when that would require resources we don't have. Do we know of suitably anti-authoritarian feminist counselors and therapy programs, and can we pay for them when the person called out can't? Can we enforce our wishes on someone who isn't cooperative—and as anarchists, should we? What consequences can we enact that actually matter? In a transient subculture, can we realistically commit to following up with someone for years into the future, and establishing structures of support and accountability that will last that long?

One phrase commonly used in survivor demands and support discourse is "safe space," that ever-elusive place in which survivors will be able to feel comfortable and fully reintegrated into collective life. What does safety mean? Is it something that we can promise? From reading the policies of recent anarchist gatherings, it appears that the primary method of securing safe space involves excluding people who have harmed others. But safety means more than quarantining those who have ruptured it for particular people, since rape culture and patriarchy suffuse all of our lives—they're not just the result of a few bad apples. While exclusion can shield survivors from the stress of sharing space with people who've harmed them, and help to protect folks in our community from repeatedly abusive people, exclusion falls painfully short of safety. In fact we may rely on banning others from spaces less because it keeps people safe than because it's one of the only safety related demands we can actually enforce.

In the essay "Safety is an Illusion," Angustia Celeste condemns the "false promises of safe space":

> *We can't provide survivors safe space; safe space in a general sense, outside of close friendships, some family and the occasional affinity, just doesn't exist... there is no such thing as safe space under patriarchy or capitalism in light of all the sexist, hetero-normative, racist, classist (etc.) domination that we live under. The more we try and pretend safety can exist at a community level, the more disappointed and betrayed our friends and lovers will be when they experience violence and do not get supported.*

What would genuine safety for survivors and for all of us look like? Are there other strategies in that direction that we can enact beyond exclusion and ostracism?[1]

4) We lack skills in counseling, mediation, and conflict resolution. Often survivor demands include finding a counselor or mediator. To be effective, this person should be willing to work for free or on a sliding scale; hold anti-authoritarian politics and a survivor-conscious feminist analysis; have the time and energy to take an active role in working with someone over a long period of time; and be close enough to the community to understand its norms, without being directly involved in the situation. How many of these people are there? How many of us even have basic active listening skills, let alone the ability to navigate complex dynamics of consent and assault, patriarchal conditioning, antiauthoritarian conflict resolution, and psychological transformation? And for those few who do fit the bill, or at least come close, how many aren't already swamped and overwhelmed?

Perhaps this is everyone's fault for not collectively prioritizing these skill sets. Fine, but what do we do right now? And how do we avoid creating a division of labor where folks with a certain set of skills or lingo become akin to authorities within anarchist versions of judicial processes?

5) This stuff depresses people and burns them out. It's intense, emotionally draining work to engage in community accountability, often with little appreciation or compensation. It can be exhausting and unrewarding, particularly when the processes rarely succeed in keeping a community intact while satisfying all participants. The gravity of the work scares people off, and understandably so.

This isn't to say that we should try to make community accountability for sexual assault and abuse fun and lighthearted. But we need to acknowledge that this is a barrier to people stepping up and staying committed for the long-term involvement we're saying is necessary for success. And these problems are magnified when we rely on skills and experience that only a few people in our circles have.

6) Accountability processes suck up disproportionate time and energy. None of us signed up for anarchy because we love participating in exhausting, interminable processes to address the stupid ways people hurt each other within our subcultural bubbles. We became anarchists because we hate cops, because we love punk shows, because we want a freer world, and for a million other reasons. When we spend so much time and energy trying to resolve internal conflicts and convince intransigent sexists to take responsibility for changing their behavior, we risk cutting ourselves off from the passions that brought us together in the first place.

It's easy to get demoralized about anarchist politics when we can't even stop assaulting each other, let alone smash the state and abolish capitalism. It's not that working to end sexual assault and patriarchy is not revolutionary - on the contrary! But if accountability processes particularly frustrating and unsuccessful ones - come to occupy too much of our collective energy, we're not likely to stay engaged and bring new folks into our struggles.

We can't sweep assault and abuse under the rug and silence survivors in the name of false unity. This previous norm perpetuated oppression and made us less effective all around, prompting community accountability efforts to emerge in the first place. We have to find a way to deal with our abusive behavior that doesn't swallow up all of our energy and demoralize us.

7) Subcultural bonds are weak enough that people just drop out. Bear in mind that many of the less coercive models of restorative justice on which community accountability frameworks are based originated in smaller-scale indigenous societies, with stronger social and cultural affinities than most any of us in the current United States can imagine. The notion that we should attempt to preserve the community and allow folks who've hurt others to remain integrated into it relies on the assumption that all parties are invested enough in this "community" to endure the scrutiny and difficult feelings that accompany going through an accountability process. The affinities that draw people into punk and anarchist scenes often aren't strong enough to keep people rooted when they feel threatened by what they're asked to do. Folks who've been called out often just pick up and leave town, sometimes even preemptively before they're called to account for their shitty behavior. Short of communicating with similar social networks in the assaulter's new destination (which happens increasingly often), there's not much we can do to prevent that. When the primary consequences we can exact for noncompliance with accountability demands involve forms of ostracism and exclusion, people will avoid these by skipping town or dropping out.[2]

8) Collective norms encourage and excuse unaccountable behavior. Our individual choices always occur in a social context, and some of the collective norms of anarchist scenes facilitate, if not directly justify, kinds of behavior that have often led to boundary-crossing and calling out.

For example, in many anarchist scenes, a culture of intoxication predominates and most social gatherings center around alcohol and drug use. Few safeguards exist when folks drink or use to excess, and few alternative spaces exist for those who want to stop or reduce their drinking or using without losing their social lives. Humor and conversation norms reinforce the notion that extreme drunkenness is normal and funny, and that people are less responsible for their actions while drunk then while sober. Weekend after weekend, we create highly sexualized spaces with strong pressure to get intoxicated, resulting in groups of people too drunk or high to give or receive solid consent.[3] Then in the aftermath of the harm caused in those situations, we expect individuals to deal with the consequences of their choices on their own, rather than all of us taking responsibility for the collective context that normalizes their behavior.

Of course, none of these dynamics excuse abuse. But sexual assault takes place in a social context, and communities can take or avoid responsibility for the kinds of behavior our social norms encourage. Alcohol and drug use is just one example of a group norm that excuses unaccountable behavior. Other entrenched dynamics that folks seeking accountability have cited as hindering their efforts include the idolization of scene celebrities (people in popular bands, renowned activists, etc.); the notion that sexual and romantic relationships are "private" and not the business of anyone outside of them; and the belief that groups who face systematic oppression (such as queers and people of color) shouldn't "air the dirty laundry" of intra-community violence, since it could be used to further demonize them.

Are we willing to examine and challenge our group norms on a collective level, to see how they promote or discourage accountable behavior? Is it possible to hold entire scenes collectively accountable for what we condone or excuse? Attempting to hold a whole group of people accountable in some structured way would likely multiply all of the problems we experience with accountability processes oriented around a single person. Yet without acknowledging and challenging our collective responsibility, holding individuals accountable won't be enough.

9) The residue of the adversarial justice system taints our application of community accountability models. Some of the most vitriolic backlash against accountability processes has been directed at their pseudo-judicial nature.

On the one hand, folks who've harmed others rarely have experience being called to account for their behavior except via authoritarian systems; attempts to do so often prompt accusations of "witch-hunts,""authoritarianism," and cop/judge/lawyer/prison guard-like behavior. Previously anti-state militants often do miraculous turnarounds, suddenly becoming extremely interested in the US government's guarantees of "justice": "Whatever happened to innocent until proven guilty, man? Don't I get a fair trial? Can't I defend myself? Listen to my character witnesses!"

On the other hand, folks pursuing accountability have received similar conditioning into adversarial conflict resolution, so it can be very easy to fall into that mode of framing the process—especially when faced with an infuriatingly stubborn anarcho-rapist. Some participants have used accountability processes as a way to threaten consequences or leverage power over others. While this may be an understandable response to the frustration and powerlessness often felt in the aftermath of abuse and assault, it can undermine attempts to pursue nonadversarial solutions.

A damning critique of the failure of anarchist accountability processes to escape the logic of the legal system comes in a communiqué explaining why a group of women physically confronted a sexual assaulter:

> *We did what had to be done out of sheer necessity. As radicals, we know the legal system is entrenched in bu-*

llshit—many laws and legal processes are racist, classist, heterosexist and misogynist. Alternative accountability processes, much like the traditional ones, often force the survivor to relive the trauma of the assault and force her to put her reputation—a problematic concept in itself—on the line as "proof" of her credibility. They end up being an ineffective recreation of the judicial process that leaves the perpetrator off the hook, while the survivor has to live through the memory of the assault for the rest of her life. The US legal system and the alternative community-based accountability processes are simply not good enough for survivors, and certainly not revolutionary.

10) Sexual assault accountability language and methods are used in situations for which they were not intended. One example of this misapplication involves the widespread use of the principle of rape crisis survivor support specifying that supporters should "always believe the survivor." This makes perfect sense in a rape crisis organization setting, solely focused on providing emotional support and services to an individual who's experienced a form of trauma that is widely disbelieved, when being believed is instrumental to the healing process. But this doesn't make sense as a basis for conflict resolution. In rape crisis counseling settings, or when someone discloses to you as a trusted friend seeking support, the focus should remain on the needs of the survivor. But transformative justice involves taking into account the needs and thus the experiences and perspectives of all parties involved, including the person who assaulted.

This does not mean that we have to figure out who's telling the truth and who's lying; that's the residue of the adversarial system again. Nor does this mean that all perspectives are equally valid and no one is right or wrong. It does mean that to encourage someone to be accountable, we have to be willing to meet them where they're at, which means accepting that one person's experience can vary significantly from that of someone else. Being accountable requires being open to the possibility that one is wrong, or at minimum that someone else could experience the same event in a dramatically different, hurtful way. But having the survivor entirely define the operating reality may not lend itself to this mode of community accountability.

Another example of the overuse and misapplication of sexual assault accountability discourse comes when people call others into accountability processes for a wide range of behaviors that aren't sexual assault. For instance, if someone feels angry and hurt after the breakup of a nonabusive relationship, it might be tempting to frame their grievances through the lens of calling someone out and demanding accountability. It could take the form of demanding that someone be banned from certain spaces, drawing on the gravity this exerts as a common accountability process demand. It's understandable that folks who feel angry or hurt for any number of reasons might want the kind of instant validation of their feelings that can come (in some circles) from framing one's hurt and anger as a call-out requiring "accountability"—whether or not that process and language makes sense for the situation.[4]

This is dangerous not only because these terms and tactics were designed for certain types of conflicts and not others, but also because their overuse may trivialize them and lead others to treat dismissively the very serious situations of assault and abuse for which they were developed. It's encouraging that issues of sexual assault and abuse have entered so widely into the discourses of radical communities. But we should be careful to avoid generalizing the methods developed for responding to one specific set of conflicts and oppressive behaviors to other situations for which they weren't intended.

In some cases, folks frustrated by someone's problematic behavior have even felt reluctant to call the person out on it for fear of that person being labeled a "perpetrator," or of others presuming the hurtful but mild form of non-consensual behavior to have been sexual assault, and thus the person addressing it to be a "survivor." When this overuse of sexual assault accountability language dovetails with the identity politics around survivor/perpetrator and policies such as the "no perps allowed" statement, this effort to promote accountability could end up discouraging people from speaking out against other forms of crummy behavior, for fear of someone being permanently tarred with the "perp" brush rather than having a few conversations, apologizing, and reading a zine.

New Directions and Further Questions

So where do we go from here? The widespread disillusionment with accountability processes suggests that we've reached an impasse. We're proposing four possible paths to explore—not as solutions to these pitfalls so much as directions for experimenting to see if they can lead to something new.

Direction 1: Survivor-Led Vigilantism

> ***"I wanted revenge. I wanted to make him feel as out of control, scared and vulnerable as he had made me feel. There is no safety really after a sexual assault, but there can be consequences."***
>
> -Angustia Celeste, "Safety is an Illusion: Reflections on Accountability"

Two situations in which prominent anarchist men were confronted and attacked by groups of women in New York and Santa Cruz made waves in anarchist circles in 2010. The debates that unfolded across our scenes in response to the actions revealed a widespread sense of frustration with existing methods of addressing sexual assault in anarchist scenes. Physical confrontation isn't a new strategy; it was one of the ways survivors responded to their abusers before community accountability discourse became widespread in anarchist circles. As accountability strategies developed, many rejected physical confrontation because it hadn't worked to stop rape or keep people safe. The trend of survivor-led vigilantism accompanied by communiqués critiquing accountability process models reflects the powerlessness and desperation felt by survivors, who are searching for alternatives in the face of the futility of the other available options.

However, survivor-led vigilantism can be a valid response to sexual assault regardless of the existence of alternatives. One doesn't need to feel powerless or sense the futility of other options to take decisive physical action against one's abuser. This approach offers several advantages. For one, in stark contrast to many accountability processes, it sets realistic goals and succeeds at them. It can feel more empowering and fulfilling than a long, frequently triggering, overly abstract process. Women can use confrontations to build collective power towards other concerted anti-patriarchal action. Physical confrontation sends an unambiguous message that sexual assault is unacceptable. If sexual violence imprints patriarchy on the bodies of women, taking revenge embodies female resistance. Above all, it's unmediated; as the author of the article "Notes on Survivor Autonomy and Violence" wrote:

> *A common criticism of accountability processes of all varieties is their tendency to mirror some sort of judicial system—structured mediation toward rehabilitation or*

punishment of one kind or another. While an outcome dictated by the survivor is certainly not akin to one dictated by the state, the process remains a mediation. Conversely, to move away from this judiciary is to reject mediation, a remnant of the idea that our interactions must be somehow guided by third parties, even third parties we choose ourselves. To that end, an attack on one's rapist is unmediated and direct, precisely that which any judicial system forbids; the line between desire and action is erased.

Of course, there are plenty of disadvantages to vigilantism, too. Choosing to escalate the situation brings serious risks, both legally and physically. Cops are more likely to bring charges for a group physical assault on a man than an "alleged" sexual assault. And, as advocates for battered women know, partner violence has a very real possibility to turn deadly; more women are killed by their partners than by any other type of attacker. Beyond the immediate risks, you can't beat up a social relationship, as they say; throttling an individual scumbag doesn't do much to make anyone safer or end systematic rape culture, however satisfying it may feel to a vindicated survivor. As mentioned above, the desire to address the roots of rape culture in responding to individual assaults helped give rise to community accountability efforts in the first place.

There's also a legacy of non-survivor-accountable vigilantism, a type of male violence that has been widely identified by survivors and anarchist women as being more about masculine ego trips than promoting healing and safety. A critique of this phenomenon comes from Supporting a Survivor of Sexual Assault, a zine oriented towards male allies of survivors, in its discussion of the principle "No More Violence":

> *Is kicking a rapist's ass going to make the rape not have happened? Will his pain make the survivor's go away? Does the survivor need to be trying to chill out another out-of-control, violent man? Probably not. Since non-trans men commit the overwhelming majority (some say over 99%) of sexual assaults, men who are supporting a survivor need to be especially conscious of the impact of male violence. It is male violence that causes rape, not what ends it. Your actions must be those of ending male violence.*
>
> *We cannot speak for the responses that survivors, women in particular, may make to rape. If women, as a majority of survivors, decide to collectively respond in a way that involves violence or asking male supporters to participate in violence; that is something for women and survivors to work out for themselves. For men who are supporting a survivor, however, it is absolutely essential that you put aside your desires for masculine retribution and interrupt the cycle of male violence... It is not your responsibility, or right, to come in vigilante-style and take matters into your own hands.*

This critique influenced the decision of groups like DWOS in Minneapolis to adopt "non-violence" as a principle. Notice, however, that this critique intentionally does not apply to survivor-led vigilantism, but to unaccountable non-survivor responses.

Apologists for anarchist men attacked by survivor-led groups claim that vigilantism is authoritarian: "Accountability cannot be a one-way street or else it becomes a synonym for punitive and policing power." But as the survivor communiqués make clear, vigilantism is not a form of "accountability," at least not community accountability based on transformative justice as it's generally conceived within anarchist circles; it's an explicit rejection of it. It's not a pseudo-judicial process; it declines both state-based and non-state methods of conflict resolution in favor of a direct, unmediated response to harm. Whether or not we think it's appropriate, it shouldn't be mistaken for a form of accountability gone wrong. On the contrary, it's an intentional response to the perceived failure of accountability methods.

So long as our practices around accountability for sexual assault and abuse don't successfully meet folks' needs, vigilantism will continue, challenging anarchist advocates of transformative justice to make their ideals a reality. Should we be trying to develop sufficiently effective accountability responses so that vigilantism isn't necessary? Or should we be developing and extending our practices of survivor-led physical confrontation?

Direction 2: Prevention Through Gender-Based Organising

It's an obvious point, but worth making: instead of spending all this energy trying to figure out how to support people who've been assaulted and respond to those who assault, wouldn't it make more sense to focus on preventing all this assaulting in the first place? Easier said than done, of course. But so far, we've only discussed reactive, after-the-fact responses to forms of harm that we're assuming will continue, even as we figure out better ways to react.

To borrow the language of the nonprofit rape crisis center world, responding to assaults and working with assaulters through accountability processes falls under intervention, or tertiary prevention. Primary prevention entails preventing first-time assault and abuse through education and by shifting social, cultural, and institutional norms, while secondary prevention involves identifying risk factors associated with assault and abuse and intervening to prevent them from escalating. So we shouldn't necessarily deem responses such as accountability processes failures if sexual assaults continue in anarchist communities. Instead, we should broaden the kinds of preventative work we're doing alongside them. What might we be doing to stop all this from happening in the first place?

Outside of anarchist circles, prevention work around gender violence usually centers on education: for women, around self-defense and harm reduction; for men, around combating rape myths and taking responsibility for ending male violence; and for all, healthy communication and relationship skills. In anarchist circles, some women have mobilized around sharing self-defense skills, and a great deal of popular education (mostly led and conducted by women) has taken place around consent, communication with partners, and positive sexuality. As noted above, while this has noticeably shifted the sexual discourses used by anarchists, we need more extensive engagement with gender oppression to break entrenched patterns.

One pathway towards this deeper transformation has come through gender-based collectives, specifically men's groups focusing on changing attitudes towards sexuality and consent among men. However, with a few exceptions such as DWOS in Minneapolis, the Philly Dudes Collective, and the Social Detox zine, there has not been much visible presence in recent years of anti-sexist men's organising among anarchists. Previously in certain scenes, anti-sexist men's groups allied with autonomous women's organizing. These formations are currently out of fashion for a number of reasons, including antifeminist backlash, a certain understanding of trans and genderqueer politics that labels all gender-based organizing as essentialist and problematic, and the absorption of so many committed anti-patriarchy militants of many genders into sexual assault response and accountability work. Could forming anti-sexist men's groups to do assault and abuse prevention work in tandem with autonomous women's organizing prove fruitful as another direction in which to experiment?

This approach could offer several advantages. Creating structures to share skills for dismantling patriarchy and self-transformation might reduce problematic behaviors among participants while also providing an infrastructure for accountability responses when folks did harm others. Pre-existing men's groups allow folks to take responsibility for self-education and action against patriarchy that doesn't have to be contingent on a "perpetrator" label or "demands." And folks could be referred to groups for a wide range of behaviors that might not raise eyebrows on their own but could be warning signs of underlying patriarchal patterns, so that others can intervene before those patterns manifest in more harmful ways (i.e., secondary prevention). For once, we'd have a place to offer folks who, whether by community compulsion or self-motivation, want to "work on their shit."

But beyond just dealing with problematic behaviors, men's groups provide space for deeper relationship building, learning, political clarification, emotional intimacy, even fun. This should provide incentive for folks to get involved and stay engaged, since it's not centered solely on debilitatingly intense crisis-mode accountability work. The kinds of study, reflection, and relationship-building that take place in these groups can strengthen the other radical organizing folks are doing in anarchist scenes, leaving us with more options, skills, and people able to respond in crisis situations. And unlike many internally-focused community accountability strategies, men's groups can interact with non-anarchist individuals and groups to spread anti-patriarchal messages and practices while learning from other feminist organizing, making our efforts relevant to broader social struggles against gender violence and patriarchy.

But wait… what about this whole gender thing? Amid the current gender politics of North American anarchist scenes, it's common to view any gender-specific organizing as suspect. Isn't this just a remnant of tired identity politics, vestiges of leftist guilt, outdated essentialism, and suspiciously authoritarian practices? Don't we want to destroy the gender binary, the real root of patriarchy and gender oppression? And doesn't organizing based on gender (or assigned gender or whatever) just reinforce the patriarchal and transphobic framework we're trying to destroy?

Certainly there are difficult questions to address in determining who "counts" as a man, whether we base our understanding on self-identification or social recognition or birth assignation, where different genderqueer and trans folks fit, and figuring out who was "socialized" how. And ending hierarchy and alienation in all their forms will require strategies more liberating than identity politics. But let's be realistic: distinct patterns of oppressive behavior and power still fall pretty predictably along gender lines. If gender-based organizing can help dislodge those patterns, perhaps we must embrace that contradiction and do our best to engage with it in all its messy complexity.

Beyond the question of gendered organizing in principle, there are other possible problems with this approach. Without subscribing to the notion that there are "good" anarchist men who're not the sexual assaulters we need to worry about, we can acknowledge that the folks who might benefit most from examining their sexist behavior will likely be least inclined to participate. Also, participating in a formal men's group could be a way for sexists to gain legitimacy, diverting attention from their crappy behavior by waving their feminist ally membership cards at people who call them out. And if the focus on gender-based organizing privileges men's groups, even anti-sexist ones, over autonomous women's and/or trans organizing, that could stabilize rather than challenge patriarchal power relations in a scene.

Direction 3: Not Accountability, But Conflict Resolution

Our struggles for accountability suffer because we have so few models, methods, or skills for resolving conflicts amongst ourselves. While it's admirable that we've put so much energy into figuring out strategies for responding to assault and abuse, there are innumerable other kinds of conflict and problematic behaviors that we also need tools to address— and as we've seen, the sexual assault-specific accountability methodologies aren't appropriate in dissimilar situations. What if we prioritized building our conflict resolution and mediation skills?

Of course, there are specific issues relevant to sexual assault and abuse, and these shouldn't be eclipsed in a general focus on conflict resolution. But if there's a precedent, language, and skill set for addressing a wide range of conflicts and harm, and being asked to participate in a conflict resolution process becomes common and less threatening, perhaps we'll be able to respond less defensively when we learn that our actions have hurt others. Rather than extending the identity politics of survivor and perpetrator, we could create more nuanced language that neither idealizes nor demonizes people, but asks all of us to remain engaged in lifelong processes of self-transformation. This requires empathy towards folks who have done harm, to create space for them to own up to their behaviors and heal.[5]

What are the advantages of framing sexual assault accountability processes within a broader emphasis on conflict resolution? There would be no need for a definitional hierarchy or litmus test to determine what "counts" as serious assault or abuse. By setting a precedent of collective engagement with less intense conflict, we would gain valuable experience to serve us in crisis situations. Framing conflict resolution as a collective responsibility could prevent the emergence of a specialized class of people who always facilitate these processes, and make it easier to find supporters with sufficient distance from a situation to be able to mediate neutrally.[6]

One cautionary point needs to be made very clearly: mediation is not appropriate for many cases of partner abuse. The article "Thinking Through Perpetrator Accountability" lays it out:

Mediation should not be used as a substitution for an accountability process. Mediation is for two people having a conflict that needs to be resolved; abuse is not mutual. Abuse is not simply about two people needing to come to the table to work things out. Mediators may certainly be useful for helping to facilitate some of the concrete negotiations within an accountability process, but please do not suggest a session with a mediator as an option instead of a long-term commitment to an accountability process.

Counselors for domestic violence survivors learn that "couples counseling" should not be undertaken in a clear situation of partner abuse, because abusers will usually manipulate the process, leaving the abusive and unequal dynamics underlying the relationship unaddressed. This is important to bear in mind so that a shift to a conflict resolution framework isn't applied to situations of abusive relationships.

What about other disadvantages? Well, there's still the problem of responding to existing problems by prescribing solutions that demand skills or resources we don't have. What can we do in the meantime, while undertaking the long-term work of learning how to resolve our conflicts? Survivors might feel frustrated to see assault and abuse lumped in with less intense or politically significant conflicts, minimizing the harm they've experienced. Asking survivors to use less forceful language when addressing perpetrators could reinforce the survivor blaming messages that they are overreacting, that sexual assault is not a significant issue worth naming strongly. Also, male "experts" in conflict resolution could hijack survivor support work and divert its feminist focus. We must acknowledge the specific context of sexual assault and abuse, honor the pain and rage of survivors, and account for oppressive power while broadening the range of conflicts we can address.

Direction 4: Concentric Circles of Affinity

> ***"There is no such thing as accountability within radical communities because there is no such thing as community,—not when it comes to sexual assault and abuse. Take an honest survey sometime and you will find that we don't agree. There is no consensus. Community in this context is a mythical, frequently invoked and much misused term. I don't want to be invested in it anymore."***
>
> -Angustia Celeste, "Safety is an Illusion: Reflections on Accountability"

At the heart of all of these questions lies one unresolved problem: what is "community?" Are we in one together as anarchists? As punks? As people in a certain local scene? Because we're at the same protest, show, or mass mobilization? Do we choose to be in it, or are we in it whether we like it or not, regardless of how we identify? And who decides all of this?

You can't have community accountability without community. The entire transformative justice framework falls apart without some coherent sense of what community means. But unfortunately, no one seems to be able to answer this question for our milieu. And without an answer, we find ourselves banging our heads against the wall again and again, when a slimy assaulter just skips town or drops out of the scene after being called out, or when someone wields enough power in a scene to gerrymander the boundaries of community to exclude survivors and allies. This is not an abstract question: it's fundamental to what we do and how power operates in our scenes.

Community becomes concrete through specific institutions, such as the websites, gatherings, social centers, and collective houses that comprise the North American anarchist scene. Although no one is taking attendance (except possibly the FBI), and many of us quarrel about who counts as a real anarchist, those of us who move through these spaces have a sense of being a part of something. We weave together this sense through shared practices that mark us as teammates: dress and body modification, quirks of diet and hygiene, conversation with specialized lingo and points of reference.

But is being a part of an anarchist "milieu" enough of a basis for the kind of community demanded by these accountability strategies? Can we realistically apply these models to our diffuse, fragmented, mostly unstructured associations of misfits?

As we move through our lives navigating connections with friends, neighbors, and comrades, we're not just part of a single unitary community, or even a web of multiple communities. Rather, our relationships with others take the form of concentric circles of affinity. From these, we can trace a tentative model to imagine how to apply community accountability models to anarchist scenes.

One of the major flaws in our notion of anarchist community lies in its nature as implicit and assumed, rather than explicit and articulated. We don't often directly state our commitments to and expectations of the other people with whom we share various kinds of "community," except in specific projects or collectives; for instance, by living together, housemates agree to pay bills on time, wash the dishes, and respect each other's space. What if we extended that degree of explicit intention to all of our relationships of affinity? Impossible: we're supposed to sit down with every anarchist in North America—or even just in our town—and spell out explicit standards for how we relate and what we expect from each other?

No, of course not… and that's exactly the point. We can't do that, so we have to figure out how to collectively determine these things within the different webs of relationships in our lives. Rather than presuming a "community" and attempting to hold people accountable based on that fiction, we should define our expectations of and commitments to the others in our various circles of affinity, and use them as the basis for our responses to conflict and harm.

For example, let's say that as my innermost concentric circle I have my affinity group. These are the folks I trust the most, with whom I take risks and for whom I'll do whatever it takes. I'd be willing to give these people the benefit of the doubt in resolving conflict and addressing harm far more than any other people. Under this model, I would sit down with my affinity group and preemptively discuss how to address conflicts with each other when they come up, ranging from the most minor to the most serious disputes and forms of harm. Think of it as a sort of pre-nuptial agreement for friends and comrades, covering the bases in case things should go wrong. That way, I have a clear sense of how to respond when one of my crew does me wrong, and a shared basis of trust for working with them in a potentially long-term process of transformation. While I wouldn't extend that trust to most people, within this group we share a deep and explicit affinity, so I'll be open to criticism, calling out, and transformation with the trust that my comrades will be, too. Other examples of this innermost circle of affinity might be families (birth or chosen), houses and land projects, various types of collectives, or tight-knit groups of friends.

The next circle outwards might be a shared community space, such as an infoshop or social center. It's a fairly consistent group of people, some of whom I'm closer with than others, but also an open space, so folks may come that I don't know. Since it's not a totally fixed group and not every single person can or would settle on direct agreements with one another, there can be collective agreements around respect, consent, antioppression, use of resources, and such. These don't have to be authoritarian; they can be collectively determined, revised at any time by the consent of those most affected, and no one is compelled to abide by them; folks who can't or won't can choose not to participate in the space. As a result, I would be willing to go along with trying to hold someone accountable insofar as they wanted to continue to participate in the space. Since what defines our "community"—the terms of our affinity with each other—is our shared experience of participation in the space, then if one of us ceases to participate in it, we're no longer in community with one another, thus shouldn't expect to be held or hold others accountable through it. And accordingly, if someone violates or refuses to abide by the collective standards, there's a procedure in place by which someone can be held accountable for their actions; and if they refuse, others can exclude them from the space in good conscience. Other examples of this second circle of affinity could include specific events, larger organizing projects, and folks who hang out loosely in shared social spaces.

This framework of concentric circles of affinity helps us imagine where we can best apply the accountability practices with which we've been experimenting these past few years among anarchists. As the circles move outwards to mass mobilizations, "anarchists," "punks," and our broader radical "community," it's harder to imagine how we could concretely define community and navigate accountability within it. There's no reason to expect anyone to be "accountable" to us based on whatever abstraction we claim to share with them. Without a concrete basis, our "community" has neither carrot nor stick; we can't reward people for going along with our demands and we can't coerce them into doing so. So if some random person who's supposedly an anarchist sexually assaults someone, it might not be realistic to approach our response to the situation in terms of community accountability.

So then what do we do? Call the cops, beat them up, kick them out of all the institutions controlled by folks with whom we share affinity? And how do we deal with the recurrent problem of people who leave one scene only to resume abusive behavior in another? We don't have any clear answers. But we have to start having discussions in every circle of affinity about our terms of engagement and how to address harm and resolve conflict, before we're in crisis and forced to figure it out as we go. Until we've done that thoroughly in every collective, space, social group, and other anarchist formation, we can't realistically aspire to formal community accountability as a strategy for dealing with our shit.

Forming affinity groups is a crucial part of anarchist organizing. It can be as simple as pulling together a crew of friends to do an action, or as formal and structured as you can imagine. Crucially, it preserves the basic principle of voluntary association at the heart of anarchy, the idea that we can do what we want with whomever we want without coercion or bureaucracy. This simple process has formed the core of our actions at demos and mobilizations, but perhaps we can use it to conceptualise our entire anarchist community and milieu. If we can create stronger ties with each other and understand our affinities more concretely, perhaps we'll have the basis to make community accountability something more than a vague and contentious dream.

We hope this essay will contribute to self-reflection among anarchists about where our affinities really are. Perhaps we can address many of the pitfalls of our experiments with accountability processes thus far by making our expectations of and commitments to one another as explicit as possible. We also can consider extending survivor-led vigilantism, pursuing antisexist men's groups and gender-based organizing to undermine rape culture, or broadening our focus on conflict resolution and mediation. Whatever paths we choose, anarchists must continue trying whatever we can to break this impasse around abuse and assault in our scenes. Our liberation depends on it.

PART 2: RETRIBUTION

"I think its time to abandon these false linguistic games we play and go back to the old model. I miss the days when it was considered reasonable to simply kick the living shit out of people and put them on the next train out of town- at least that exchange was clear and honest".

– Angustia Celeste, "Safety is an Illusion: Reflections on Accountability"

So on the one side, we have approaches based on dialogue. On the other, we have tactics of coercion. Those really are our choices in a nutshell. Retribution, retaliation, revenge; all involve returning some harm to - or imposing sanctions on - the perpetrator. This is never going to be pleasant or easy, but given the long anarchist history of direct action, it is surprising how often survivor-led responses are not considered in the same light. Instead they are often flippantly dismissed as 'authoritarian', 'vigilante', 'reactionary', or 'emotional'.

Far from negating these acts as 'emotional', we need to acknowledge that they are rooted in very real and legitimate desires; safety, catharsis, healing, and empowerment of the oppressed in the midst of deep structural inequalities. The following statements will hopefully provide greater insight into why some people resort to these acts. The subsequent article then seeks to address some concerns about the 'reactionary-authoritarian' perception of retributive action, and consider the place of revenge in anarchist praxis.

"Anarchist" Rapist Gets the Bat: We'll Show You Crazy Bitches Part II (2010)

Submitted by Anonymous on Mon, 04/26/2010 - 07:10

jacob onto is a piece of shit rapist. we are tired of accountability processes that force the survivor to relive, over and over, the trauma of assault; that force the survivor to put their reputation on the line as "proof" of their credibility; that end up being an ineffective recreation of the judicial process that leaves the perpetrator scot free, while the survivor has to live through this for the rest of their life.

at the very least, the perpetrator should feel something, some lasting mark of his behavior, something he will remember every time he has sex – that is, if he ever has sex again. so we decided to make sure this is an assault that jacob never fucking forgets.

we rolled in with a baseball bat. we pulled his books off his shelves: he admitted it, not a single one mentioned consent. we made him say it: "i am a rapist." we left him crying in the dark on his bed: he will never feel safe there again.

this is a precedent. this is the beginning of a new kind of accountability process, one that leaves the perpetrator in pain – though this is still only a tiny fraction of the pain that he has caused. we know that jacob is not the only guilty one. we know there are more of you out there.

we are not sorry, and we will not stop: from now on, we will respond to sexual violence with violence.

"if you touch me, i will fucking kill you." let the roundups begin.

(a public service announcement: we encourage you to all use consent from here on out. and let it be clear: consent is not the absence of a 'no,' but the presence of a 'yes.')

i. Communique

Anon

This is an unwavering political statement, a conscious effort to politicize an event without being apologetic or defensive. This statement is written by a collective of women who came together in the spring of 2010 based on shared experiences and concerns surrounding patriarchy and sexual violence within the radical scene and beyond. In our meetings and discussions, we learned that many of the women within our network have experienced some form of sexual violence. It is no coincidence that we have had this experience with power. Rape is not a personal misfortune but an experience with domination shared by many women. When more than two people have suffered the same oppression the problem is no longer personal but political – thus, rape is a political matter.

– New York Radical Feminists Manifesto, 1971

Violence against women contributes to a system of power, organizing society into a complex set of relationships based on a sometimes invisible and internalized assumption of male supremacy. Rape is not the only form of control that male-bodied individuals can practice in romantic, friendly, or comradely relationships. Physical as well as emotional abuse function as ways of maintaining involuntary hierarchies and control over women, female sexuality, and reproductive systems.

The silence and secrecy that often surrounds issues of power and domination should in no way be taken as complicity, however, we as women and survivors will remain silent no longer. Ideologically speaking, male-bodied anarchists and communists align with principles of egalitarianism and anti-authoritarianism, yet daily practices in this regard oftentimes fall short. We have repeatedly seen a chasm between theory and praxis in male-bodied treatment of women and other oppressed people. We have seen over and over again, male-gendered behaviors reproduce the very systems of domination that we are fighting to dismantle. We refuse to allow this to continue.

In the course of our meetings, we identified one male-bodied individual as a repeat perpetrator of sexual violence against female-bodied people: Jan Michael Dichter, also known as Maus. This particular individual, whose vocabulary consisted of anti-patriarchal jargon, had committed sexual violence before, and participated in survivor-defined accountability processes. Since he continued to transgress boundaries, raping and sexually assaulting women in Boston and Santa Cruz, we decided to confront him. We met him at his home and verbally confronted him. He refused to take responsibility and his words were manipulative and insulting. When he refused to shut up, we shut him up. The intent was to inflict pain, albeit it would only be a small portion of the amount of pain his victims have felt.

We did what had to be done out of sheer necessity. As radicals, we know the legal system is entrenched in bullshit

– many laws and legal processes are racist, classist, heterosexist and misogynist. Alternative accountability processes, much like the traditional ones, often force the survivor to relive the trauma of the assault and force her to put her reputation – a problematic concept in itself – on the line as "proof" of her credibility. They end up being an ineffective recreation of the judicial process that leaves the perpetrator off the hook, while the survivor has to live through the memory of the assault for the rest of her life (Anonymous communiqué from NYC, 2009). The US legal system and the alternative community-based accountability processes are simply not good enough for survivors, and certainly not revolutionary.

Rape is entangled in a system of patriarchy and domination. It would serve us well to consider rape as part of class and race analysis. It is not only a crime committed by individuals against individuals; it is systemic and structual. It is our material interest as women that pushes us to stand up for ourselves.

The material consequences of patriarchy and male supremacy push all women, regardless of how they define themselves ideologically, to fight against our oppression. In our work as a radical community, both female- and male-bodied, we must work to dismantle this form of oppression and domination. We find it an incomprehensible and unacceptable betrayal that our so-called male-bodied 'friends' would perpetrate this kind of subjugation of female-bodied comrades. Just because you can articulate feminist theory does not mean that you are to be trusted.

We also find tacit support of male-bodied perpetrators, as well as the hijacking of our collectively defined accountability process particularly offensive. Attempts by some self-identified "male allies" to take control of the action by confronting Maus themselves, pressuring women for inclusion and calling a public meeting without our permission undermined our practice of self-organization. Rather than demonstrating their support these men made it clear that they were unwilling to allow us to act on our own behalf without their involvement. The type of action we took as a group of female-bodied comrades aligns clearly with anti-hierarchical politics and goals of self determination. If our male-bodied 'comrades' want to be considered as comrades, we'd like to see them behave that way.

This action sets a precedent, the beginning of a new kind of accountability process, one that leaves the perpetrator in pain and articulates our call for the dismantling of male supremacy in radical political communities and beyond. We know that Maus is not the only guilty one. We know there are more of you out there...

It would take a revolution to eliminate structural violence; thus an antirape agenda must be part of any revolutionary agenda. We demand this now.

Beyond Revenge & Reconciliation: demolishing the straw men

(a)legal

This piece sets out conclusions drawn from concerns about transformative and retributive justice (eg. accountability processes and acts of revenge, respectively), expressed in the previous articles and elsewhere. It calls for a flexible, critical approach to dealing with abuses of power & domination in our communities, so as to be as effective as possible in fighting these hierarchies. It suggests that we need accountable processes, that is, 'accountability processes' themselves, and any other methods we use, wherever possible have safeguards against their abuse, and impede the colonisation of a new morality. Finally, it argues that we should be developing a range of tools for dealing with these problems, both responsive and preventative in nature. A number of specific ideas are proposed at the end of the article.

Dealing with our Dogmas

Retributive Justice

Transformative justice's power derives in part from its fundamental opposition to retributive justice. Retributive justice simply involves responding to a transgression with some kind of harm, and can include anything from capital punishment, prisons and community service; vigilante campaigns by civilian militias (i.e. dominant social groups working to complement to state justice); or survivor-led action designed to injure, shame or otherwise penalise an abuser (eg. denying them privileges or requiring them to undertake certain duties).

Despite its varied incarnations, talk of retribution frequently provokes hostile reactions in activist circles, at least in English-speaking quarters. Its status as the harshest weapon of the state against its domestic population (although it has now added restorative justice to its armoury) has led to a rejection of all forms of retaliation, a sentiment expressed in particular by those with liberal tendancies who are unable to envisage the power to exact potentially violent revenge in the hands of the oppressed, or consider this to be as oppressive as the transgression itself. As the communiqués in this zine and our own anarchist histories show, however, there will always be groups and individuals who respond to their oppression with action rather than dialogue.

Frequently underlying the dismissal of retribution is the assumption that violence can never be justified – even though revenge may not necessarily assume violent form. Survivor-led retaliation that subverts the social order has been conflated with state-dispensed 'justice' and vigilantism by reactionary groups seeking to preserve the status quo. The rejection also arguably lies in the role some NGOs have played in advocating transformative & restorative justice over direct action by survivors. This is no doubt due in part to the unpredictable, potentially illegal, and deeply personal manifestations of revenge, and that this knowledge is not easily imparted through roleplays and powerpoint slides. As such, it is less amenable to dogma. Despite their good motivations, sadly, it is often the case that when funded organisations take it upon themselves to deliver training on resistance, privilege, consensus, accountability, and so on, certain principles tend to become gospel in the absence of a strong critical analysis built into the content of the training. Many critiques of retributive action are therefore attacks on straw men and are riddled with uninterrogated liberal assumptions.

Conversely, as with transformative approaches, retribution has strong subversive potential. Violent action by oppressed groups has historical precedent for creating critical changes in their conditions. Its cathartic and liberatory aspects were articulated powerfully by anti-imperialist and psychoanalyst, Frantz Fanon, who saw it as a realisation and affirmation of the collective power of the oppressed. The revenge attacks and assassinations carried out by 19th and early 20th century anarchists helped keep anarchism alive in a time of severe repression, and inspired other comrades to find courage. Women in abusive relationships may take strength from seeing other women acting collectively to kick a rapist out of their social centre, while some people may be forced to reflect on their own problem behaviour when the expression of collective displeasure and the undesirable consequences are difficult to ignore. The unpredictability of survivor-led revenge and the strength of feeling involved helps abusers understand the risks that oppressive behaviour entails.

Various forms of retaliation are used today by anarchists against rapists, batterers and perpetrators of sexual assault, perhaps most commonly in the form of public exposure, which may involve publishing a culprit's details on the Internet or in activist spaces, or outing them publicly (in one case, a group of Italian feminists successfully interrupted a university seminar attended by a perpetrator of domestic violence and refused to leave without him). This shaming may be a secondary consequence of actions designed to warn others about the individual.

This is not to say that violent retaliation, or in fact any form of retaliation is unproblematic. In particular, using the intense power of shame (whether as a tool in itself or as a consequence of punitive action) can perpetuate unacceptable behaviour by that person and entrench undesirable ways of relating to one another. Do we want to have a culture in which we're disciplined by fear of shame and rejection? Do we want to live our lives according to norms and morality – that is, behaviour that is driven by desire for conformity – or according to values and ethics which we've thought through and chosen for ourselves? Can we use tactics against our enemies which we consider problematic for our communities, whilst rejecting those principles for ourselves? Although we may we never be able to fully free ourselves from fear of rejection and ostracism, does that mean we shouldn't at least try to challenge dominant modes of social control such as shame, conformity and respect for hierarchy? After all, this is arguably just as much, if not a more powerful, mainstay of the oppressive status quo than fear of the police or the prisons.

Given the potential dangers of retaliation and punitive action, it should ideally be reserved for serious cases where reconciliation is out of the question. Another reason for this is the risk of 'getting it wrong', discussed more later. A further question is, who decides whether to take punitive action or expulsion? Ideally the project, social centre, campaign group or whichever collective the accused is part of will decide together with the survivor(s), taking into account the overall picture and the accused's patterns of behaviour. This is obviously easier said than done in some cases, as many abusers are very skilled at concealing their behaviour in public. On the other hand, it is also common to find individuals who repeat certain patterns of interaction over and over with different partners, and dominant behaviour may not confined exclusively to their intimate relationships.

Following a collective decision to act, any course of action should be survivor-centred, i.e. once it has been agreed that a person will be expelled, publicly exposed, or even attacked, the needs or desires of the survivor(s), who may have serious concerns for their own safety, should be prioritised. How and when action is carried out should be agreed with those needs at the forefront of people's minds. Ideally we would see a culture where the wider collective (rather than a group of the survivor's friends) will support direct action where appropriate. However, in cases where there is disagreement, there will always be some who choose to take retaliatory action regardless of the wider group's decision. The question for the collective will then be whether to act against those individual(s), as it is important to guard against the abuse of these processes.

Despite the potential dangers of retributive action, if used in appropriate situations and with a critical analysis of power, it may be key to establishing safety, empowering survivors, warning potential abusers, and realising the collective strength of oppressed groups.

Transformative Justice

Transformative justice offers significant opportunities for enriching our understanding of power and its abuse. This is particularly so around issues of relationships and sex, where fear, conditioning and insecurities often undermine understanding. We can seek reconciliation through formal processes of accountability, or through other means that promote dialogue. Where accountability processes fall down however – and, as the previous articles indicate, they often do fall down – it appears in part to be when they are applied uncritically and without proper consideration of alternatives.

In particular, one of the most worrying tendencies to have

emerged in some US radical scenes is the harsh dismissal of concerns about these processes. If disagreements are voiced by those assigned to a 'dominant' or 'privileged' group (eg. men), then this is taken as evidence of 'providing rhetorical cover for treating survivors like enemies' (patriarchyhaters), or 'counter-organising' (Incite!).

On the contrary, if there is one lesson we can learn from these experiments over the past few years, it is the importance of evaluating and adapting our response mechanisms. Without doing so, we run the risk of entrenching a dogmatic approach to accountability processes.

Such an approach:

– can wreak considerable destruction and infighting in a collective;

– positions transformative justice above, and in opposition to, retributive approaches, delegitimising direct action by survivors;

– conceals the fact that misgivings about retribution can often be rooted in a state-centric paradigm (states use prisons, prisons perpetuate the problem = retribution is bad);

– leads to inappropriate use of accountability processes, e.g. against those who call the processes into question;

– creates an onus to 'always believe the survivor', regardless of other dynamics going on (discussed more later);

– imposes considerable burdens on people's time and takes energy away from other important work. This burden can be particularly unreasonable in the case of single parents, those with care duties or those juggling jobs (who might also want to get on with radical projects!);

– propagates unquestioned liberal assumptions held by some of TJ's NGO champions;

– conceals the distinct (in particular, US) contexts in which they have emerged, and the tendency of US discourses to be uncritically imported into other parts of the Anglosphere (e.g. privilege theory, critical whiteness);

– undermines the distinction between those we actually want to have in our lives and communities and those we don't.

This last point, articulated by CrimethInc in the idea of 'concentric circles of affinity', is crucial to even the least undogmatic applications of transformative justice. For any process (of 'accountability' or other) to satisfy our needs and minimise their impact on our collectives, it is essential that lines are continually drawn between perpetrators we actually want to spend time on and those we don't. Possible guidelines for this are laid out in the next section. This is essential, because we may well believe that no-one is beyond help, but some people may take 10 years' hard work and support to change their behaviour. The question for us then, is really whether we want to spend many months or years of our time and energy changing individual behaviour? Do we have those kinds of resources? And is this the appropriate strategy for fighting rape and gendered violence?

As with retributive justice, 'transformative' approaches fall down in the absence of a radical analysis of power. One way of reducing the risk is by developing more nuanced and varied responses to oppressive behaviour within our communities. It is to this that we now turn.

Alternative Approaches

A. Deciding on a path

As mentioned above, before a collective opts to take any course of action, they need to decide whether or not the person accused might be able to remain in the group. This will inform whether the approach taken is one based mostly on dialogue or action. There can be no hard and fast rules on this, as every group will be coming at the issue from different angles and have different understandings of minor and severe harm, depending on the politics of the group, its focus, the experiences of its members and the personalities and inclinations of those involved.

However, a few factors, **taken together**, can be used to guide a decision:

- Reconciliation (the accused remains in the group)

- The person making allegations desires reconciliation
- The collective feels love and/or affinity for the accused
- The harm caused is relatively minor

- The harm is caused through error of judgement
- The harm is caused through ignorance
- The accused alleges or is known to have themselves suffered relevant hardship or abuse, recently or historically (i.e. they too are survivors)
- The accused denies the act and is believed (see below)
- The accused expresses remorse

• Expulsion

- The person making allegations wants the accused to leave
- The collective does not feel sufficient affinity with the accused
- The harm caused is severe
- There is a pattern of abuse
- The accused has not been responsive to dialogue
- The accused appears to have been aware that they were crossing boundaries
- The accused denies the act(s) but is disbelieved (see below)
- The accused expresses no sincere remorse

We should always be starting from a position of believing the survivor and taking steps to immediately establish their safety. Yet that does not mean that allegations can never be called into question. One key objective of accountability processes is that the accused acknowledges responsibility for the harm caused, without engaging in denial or excuses.

Accountability is in fact in many cases seen as synonymous with taking responsibility, which provides no meaningful opportunity for self-defence against those accusations. Processes are not going to invite participation if they are seen to be unfair, so we need to put checks in place to guard against processes which are themselves unaccountable and are vulnerable to misuse and abuse.

Some cases are clear cut, others much less so. A "you are either with the survivors or you're a rape apologist" attitude is unhelpful. While this is an understandable approach given the patriarchal society in which we live (in the UK, 7% of reported rapes lead to conviction), it is undeniable that some people (albeit distinct minority) do make false accusations of various kinds against others. This might be because they have an axe to grind, or because they suffer from particular mental health problems. It is also true that radical circles can be a magnet for people with such problems due to the more generally supportive culture and our systemic analyses of mental health conditions. We need to allow for the possibility that an accusation may be false, and by diving into accountability processes that require an admission of responsibility, I cannot see any way out for people caught up in such a scenario.

Reasons for the collective believing the accused's denial should be based on consideration of the overall picture, including their broader patterns of behaviour, having (where appropriate & tactfully) consulted other/previous partners about their experience of the accused; other dynamics in the relationship; and consideration, where appropriate, of other, previous unacceptable behaviour by the person making allegations (e.g. having made other allegations known to be false, inappropriately publishing people's details on the Internet, calling the police on comrades, etc.). These decisions will at times be very hard to make, but will need consideration if we are to respond appropriately to what are not always straightforward situations.

However, no-one can be expected to be an expert in this, particularly if oppressive behaviour is a relatively rare occurence in a collective. Advice may therefore be sought from elsewhere, as I discuss further below.

B. Mediation

Once it has been established that a person can remain in a given collective and that the imbalance of power is not so great as to undermine it, mediation might then be required in cases still needing 'external' intervention. Friends, the collective, and the survivor could recommend this. The scale of accountability processes mean that they are vulnerable to people taking sides and the process erupting into wider conflict in the collective/movement (especially since a lot of groups themselves are small). To avoid escalating the conflict and consuming the energy of a group that probably has other priorities, mediation may be a more suitable, smaller scale, alternative. Processes of mediation could be used involving up to three people (a skilled and relatively 'neutral' mediator, and a support person for each party), rather than accountability processes which tend to create whole 'support groups' on either side. The mediator should promote dialogue and understanding and facilitate an agreement whereby the accused will take steps to change their behaviour in cases where responsibilty for an act is acknowledged (as in accountability processes). An example of this could be attending a self-help group (below). An agreement could also be made to check in on the progress of this further down the line.

C. Self-help groups

Following mediation, or independently of it, either party could join a selfhelp group. For the accused, this may be a condition set by a collective, or an agreement reached in mediation. The concept of self-help groups for 'perpetrators' and 'survivors' - for want of better words - could form part of both a preventative and a response strategy.

Oppression awareness groups

Referrals could be made by anybody (partners, friends, collectives or the accused themselves), and participation could be for a specified time period (e.g. six months). Others wanting to unlearn patriarchal or otherwise hierarchical behaviour could participate as well. Sessions could be run collectively by participants and a handful of skilled volunteers. In an encouraging, non-judgemental environment, participants could support each other in better understanding power, hierarchy and the dynamics of abuse. Like other DIY education projects, texts could be read outside group time and discussed during sessions.

The goal would be to strengthen our communities by increasing our understanding of power and its abuse, and in turn treat each other with greater respect and comradeship. Individuals who participate may improve their behaviour, and at the same time support others in doing so. Helping/teaching others also consolidates our own knowledge and encourages us to be self-reflective.

Finally, along with survivor self help groups (see below), where appropriate these groups could be consulted in cases where a collective is considering whether to exclude an individual. The group could make suggestions, for example, on the factors to be taken into consideration when making such a decision, or how to go about approaching the accused. With the help of facilitators or counsellors, this would allow 'perpetrators' who remain in collectives to play a positive part in challenging oppressive behaviour, as well as providing checks on the misuse of accountability processes.

An advantage of this project is that those who want & need to work on these issues have a space for doing so without it necessarily dragging in people who would rather get on with other things. The self-help format, meanwhile, is designed to empower people to make change rather than shaming them into it. Again, this approach would only be appropriate for those with whom we have affinity and who we would like to remain in our communities.

'Survivor' self-help

In a similar vein, those who have suffered abusive relationships or experiences could have an opportunity to join forces and support one another. Again, they would not necessarily need to have undergone mediation or any other collective process to access these groups. As with the oppression awareness groups, they could be run by survivors/victims with the help of skilled counsellors or other supporters. The project could function as a space for listening, validation, rebuilding self-esteem, learning to identify signs of abuse and manipulation, developing the strength and skills to challenge abuse, and preparing possible ways out of a situation where necessary. Reading 'homework' and self-defence training could potentially be incorporated into these sessions.

As with the oppression awareness groups, survivor groups could also act in an advisory capacity to collectives considering how to take an allegation forward. In this way, both 'survivors' and 'perpetrators' can move from being disempowered and constrained by those labels, to having the strength and knowledge to feedback into the wider community.

Practical problems posed by these groups are issues of capacity for them to function on the local level required for regular communication, and the question of whether there would be sufficient demand. At least in relation to the oppression awareness groups, I think that the anarchist 'community' in the UK is currently too weak for them to operate locally. It might therefore make more sense to establish one or two groups (e.g. North and South) or regional groups, and for meetings to assume the form of intensive monthly gatherings bolstered by online communication, such as a mailing list. Funds can be pooled by the group to help towards the cost of travel. Survivor groups may have more demand, and might therefore be able to operate in some local areas.

Despite some logistical challenges, putting this infrastructure in place may be a worthwhile investment as both a preventative strategy and as a means of building the resilience and political integrity of our networks, as well as guarding against dogmas in accountability processes.

D. Internal resolution

Ultimately, our approaches should be geared towards building strong and resourceful individuals who are able to challenge acts of domination where possible through direct communication without requiring the input of the whole collective/project. Establishing resources such as self-help groups may help towards this.

E. Exclusion and Retribution

In cases where it is not considered appropriate for a person to remain in a collective, action will need to be taken to expel them. The harm caused having been particularly serious, at this point the goal becomes the establishment of safety, demonstrating love and solidarity with the survivor(s), and helping them to find their power. These principles have been shown to be vital to helping victims overcome trauma.

Translating those principles into action will mean expelling an individual in a way that the survivor(s) are comfortable with. They may or may not want to be involved, and may want others they particularly identify with to form part of the group that carries it out (other women/people of colour/queer/trans people etc.).

One concern is that expulsion does not 'solve' the problem, and potentially just passes it onto other groups to deal with. Yet whether or not we see this as a serious challenge depends very much on our objectives. It underscores the importance of being conscious of and flexible in those objectives (from 'transforming' the culprit, to empowering victims & establishing safety, and so on), and of not being constrained by the dogmas of different approaches. While expulsion may seem like 'giving up' or passing the problem onto others, we also have many enemies in the world who we wouldn't dream of sharing our spaces with. We need to be watchful of falling foul of the missionary complex: we have no duty to 'save' or 'transform' individuals, particularly if we feel little affiliation with them. We don't think it's worth our while trying to 'convert' cops or judges, so why would we think differently about serial abusers?

In demonstrating love and solidarity and helping to empower survivors, the collective or another group including the survivor may want to take other actions, such as publicly exposing the culprit, attacking their property, or causing them physical harm. The important thing here is that the survivor(s) are satisfied and given the power and respect to take action. Again, to avoid 'getting it wrong', in cases where the perpetrator is a member of the community/collective this should ideally only be on the cards where the group has reached the decision that that the individual cannot be reconciled, i.e. the decision has been carefully considered beforehand.

Conclusion

No process is going to be free of pain and distress, but if we are to have some degree of satisfaction with their outcomes whilst minimising their impact on our collectives, we need to forgo dogmatism, question our assumptions & objectives, and critically experiment with a range of tools.

Further Reading

Most of the following resources are available online:

Alex Gorrion et al.The Broken Teapot (critique of TJ)
Angustia Celeste, Safety is an Illusion: Reflections on Accountability
Bay Area Transformative Justice Collective (list of resources)
www.batjc.wordpress.com
Community Accountability: ideas, actions, art, & resources for communities responding to & transforming violence - resources
www.communityaccountability.wordpress.com
Ching-In Chen et al. The Revolution Starts at Home: confronting intimate violence within activist communities (Book)
Ching-In Chen et al. The Revolution Starts at Home: confronting partner abuse in activist communities (Zine)
Christine Sivell-Ferri et al. The Four Circles of Hollow Water. Aboriginal Peoples Collection.
Creative Interventions, Creative Interventions Toolkit: A Practical Guide to Stop Interpersonal Violence [pre-release version 06.2012]
Critical Resistance and INCITE!, 'Women of Color against Violence Statement on Gender Violence and the Prison Industrial Complex'
Generation FIVE, Toward Transformative Justice: A Li-

beratory Approach to Child Sexual Abuse and other forms of Intimate and Community Violence

Judith Herman, Trauma and Recovery: The Aftermath of Violence - from Domestic Abuse to Political Terror (Book)

INCITE! Women of Color Against Violence, 'Community Accountability: Principles/Concerns/Strategies/Models Working Document'

Philly Survivor Support Collective, 'Strategies for Survivors' (Philly Survivor Support Collective: 9 April 2013)

Ravachol et al. Vive l'Anarchie!: Illegalist Trial Statements (anarchists on crime & vengeance)

SOA Watch Taking The First Step: Suggestions To People Called Out For Abusive Behavior

Various. What do we do when? A zine about community response to sexual assault, Issue 2

Various, Dangerous Spaces: violent resistance, self-defense, and insurrectional struggle against gender

List of projects doing work around TJ/related issues at www.phillystandsup.org

List (& online copies) of zines dealing with sexual assault and community accountability at www.phillyspissed.net

Big thanks to the comrades who shared their thoughts and experiences on these issues and supported & inspired me to put this collection together. Much love to you.

Copies of this zine can be accessed online at
www.dysophia.org.uk

More copies of this pocketbook and many other anarchist books and texts are available from
Active Distriution Mailorder
www.activedistributionshop.org